THE CHURCH

IN THE

WILDERNESS

Mike Warriner

The Church
❯— in the —❮
Wilderness

A Message to Today's Church

Tate Publishing & *Enterprises*

Published by Tate Publishing & Enterprises, LLC
127 E. Trade Center Terrace | Mustang, Oklahoma 73064 USA
1.888.361.9473 | www.tatepublishing.com

Tate Publishing is committed to excellence in the publishing industry. The company reflects the philosophy established by the founders, based on Psalm 68:11,
"The Lord gave the word and great was the company of those who published it."

Book design copyright © 2008 by Tate Publishing, LLC. All rights reserved.
Cover design by Nathan Harmony
Interior design by Jacob Crissup

Published in the United States of America

ISBN: 978-1-60462-948-4
1. Christian Living: Practical Life: Contemporary Issues
2. Church & Ministry: Church Life: Church Growth & Renewal
08.04.24

DEDICATION

To my precious gift from God, my wife, Regina, and to my father, Frank, who went to Glory before he saw the final copy

Table of Contents

Introduction

First of all, I need to tell you who I am. Fortunately, that will take few words. I am nobody. I am not the pastor of a huge, highly successful church or a famous television personality. My singing voice is a "joyful noise," and you have never heard me on the radio. My job experience is in construction, hotels, street ministry, and driving a big truck. In short, each of you is probably a more likely candidate to bring this message than I—an issue I have brought before the Lord many times.

My desire, when I came to my senses and returned to my Father's house like the prodigal in Luke 15:17-18, was to tell others about his grace and mercy so that they may find the peace and joy that I had found. I prayed that God would bring the lost across my path so that I might win some to the kingdom. His answer to my prayer was both unexpected and disconcerting. He showed me that if I could win every person that I saw it would be a very small number in the overall scheme of things, but if I would remind his church of its true calling, millions would be saved. He spoke to me through the Book of Ezekiel, showing me that as Israel had strayed so had the church. The Lord directed me to take his message to the church, a people who spoke the same language.

> He then said to me: "Son of man, go now to the house of Israel and speak my words to them. You are not being sent to a people of obscure speech and difficult language, but to the house of Israel-- not to many peoples of obscure speech and difficult language, whose words you cannot understand. Surely if I had sent you to them, they would have listened to you. But the house of Israel is not willing to listen to you because they are not willing to listen to me, for the whole house of Israel is hardened and obstinate. But I will make you as unyielding and hardened as they are. I will make your forehead like the hardest stone, harder than flint. Do not be afraid of them or terrified by them, though they are a rebellious house." And he said to me, "Son of man, listen carefully and take to heart all the words I speak to you. Go now to your countrymen in exile and speak to them. Say to them, 'This is what the Sovereign LORD says,' whether they listen or fail to listen."
>
> Ezekiel 3:4-11 (NIV)

Frankly, the thought of witnessing to individuals caused me to shudder, so the idea of speaking before a church was beyond comprehension. I was, however, filled with a ravenous hunger to consume the Word of God. A wonderful woman of God, Fuscia Pickett, spoke at a seminar I attended about her "teacher," the Holy Spirit, who opened the truth of the Word to her. Calling upon the Holy Spirit to teach me was a monumental step in my studies. He is so faithful to guide us to truth and to bring light to the mysteries of life to all who ask. This experience of learning at the feet of the Holy Spirit gave me understanding of Psalm 51:11 when David pleaded that the Holy Spirit not be taken from him. His presence, guidance, and counsel are more precious than anything on earth.

Shortly after my return to the Lord, my thoughts were constantly filled with the question, "Greater things than these shall you do in my name. Why aren't they being done?"

"I don't know, Lord," was my response.

He told me he would show me. Seven years later, my Teacher had guided me through the Old Testament ("to know the God you serve"), the Gospels ("to know My Son, Jesus Christ"), and the rest to show me the function of the Holy Spirit and to introduce me to the church. The purpose of this journey was to see the church as Jesus had established it and the reasons why it was done as it was done. Again, that was a seven-year journey that brought me back to that frightening place of taking his message to the church.

After seven years of teaching, the Lord led me to Australia on what I thought would be an evangelistic mission trip. Nine months later I realized that this, too, had been training. My Teacher showed me that the whole church, wherever it may be found, needed to hear the message. I next spent three years in the wilderness of over-the-road truck driving where my Teacher used the solitude of away-from-home driving to continue to prepare me as a messenger. My greatest fear was that I would fail and be humiliated. Now I realize the pride in that attitude. It is his message, not mine. Whether it is heard or not is his providence, not mine. Whatever action or reaction occurs is in his hands. I just thank him that I can serve him as a messenger.

I am nobody who has been forgiven much and, because of God's grace and mercy given to me, has the honor of calling Almighty God, Creator of the Universe, my Father. This is the message to the church he has given me to deliver. Oh, God, let me be faithful and humble in obedience to you. My prayer for those who may read this message is simple:

Almighty God, Perfect Father, Teacher, open our eyes to see and ears to hear. Give us a soft heart ready to change as you give direction. Fix this message in our spirit so that we may know the urgency and importance that you intend from your words. May we become one as our Savior and you are one.

Guide us, your people and your bride, out of the wilderness so that we may become your glory. In the name of Jesus we pray, Amen.

THE VISIONS

Shortly after the Lord gave me the first inkling of my call as a messenger to his church, I was given a vision while praying and fasting at a secluded mountain site on the island of Kauai. The Teacher showed me a spire like the top of an obelisk. It was filthy, covered with soot, dust, and cobwebs. Soon a white cloud engulfed this spire and completely covered it. When the cloud moved away the spire had been totally cleansed. It sparkled in the sun, and one could tell it was made of the finest crystal imaginable. A voice spoke from the cloud and said, "I will clean my church." Then my vision was expanded to see miles of crystal buildings and spires, all sparkling in the light. This vision was followed within a few weeks by a second one.

The second vision occurred while meditating on the first vision and placed me at a vantage point looking at a path that ran down a valley between two mountains.

There was a third mountain in the background that caused the path to turn right to go around it. As my eyes followed the path around the mountain I was led into a desert landscape, totally barren and sloping into a vast valley. In front of me, in this wilderness, I saw a cloud of dust like that kicked up by movement in dry places, and I saw a large gathering of people—hundreds, thousands, even tens of thousands—plodding endlessly to and fro. Then I saw a column moving toward me, five or six people wide, stretching back to the throng. I heard music in the heavens above me that can only be described as victorious. I was taken back to the original viewpoint, but higher. From this position I could see the path all the way into the wilderness and back to the throng. As the front lines of the column made their way around the mountain in the background and came straight up the path between the other two mountains, I could see the individuals in the column. They looked as if they had been through a mighty conflict—clothes in rags, bloodstains on their bodies. I was drawn to their faces; there was no conflict there. These were the faces of over-comers—strong, courageous, and beaming with hope. The music became louder and more victorious. My attention was pulled from these faces to the slopes of the mountains. There I saw small bushes and trees, barely large enough to provide shade. All over the slopes, hidden under these plants, were people. I wondered why I hadn't seen them before. They were sheltered by ragged tents and blankets, and I could see that most of them were wounded, crippled, and nearly dead. Then I saw some of those in the column begin to move into the scrub, to direct those who could walk and to carry those who couldn't, out to join the march. The column never slowed but continued to move forward.

I was drawn to one older man who used a home-made crutch as he tried to get down the slope. Soon, two from the column came and placed this man's arms on their shoulders and helped him to the ranks. It seemed significant that his crutch fell to the ground as the two supported him. When they had returned to the column, the two continued to support this man. I watched as his face began to glow and take on that same look of victory and hope of those around him. He grew stronger with each step and was soon marching on his own. The music now was as if every instrument that had ever been made was being played in perfect tune by the greatest musicians ever heard. The final view was of this column passing beneath me but stretching all the way back into the desert.

The last vision I will share with you sealed in my spirit the resolve to continue to seek his time and place for me to serve him. I was given a glimpse into the throne-room of our Lord. There I saw my Savior weeping as he watched the thousands of lost souls passing his throne—those who rejected his gift of life. I was reminded that he gave his life for us when we hated him so that his love could draw us to eternal life with him. I wept as I understood my Lord grieves over every soul who refuses his sacrifice.

THE WILDERNESS:

WHERE WE ARE

As my eyes followed the path around the mountain I was led into a desert landscape, totally barren and sloping into a vast valley. In front of me, in this wilderness, I saw a cloud of dust like that kicked up by movement in dry places, and I saw a large gathering of people—hundreds, thousands, even tens of thousands—plodding endlessly to and fro.

There is a place in Scripture called the wilderness. It is a place of both physical and spiritual importance. The wilderness was used for escape, refuge, punishment, temptation discouragement, and revelation. God took the Israelites into the wilderness when he delivered them from the oppression of the Pharaoh in Egypt. Because of their unbelief he kept them in the wilderness for an extra forty years until the rebellious first generation had all died, then the next generation entered into the promised land. Before God called out to Moses from the burning bush to lead his people from captivity, he had already been in the wilderness for forty years hiding for the murder he had committed in Egypt as the Pharaoh's grandson. David and his mighty men used the wilderness as a refuge and stronghold while King Saul tried to kill them. Elijah fled from Queen Jezebel into the wilderness in discouragement and asked God to let him die there. John the Baptist came out of the wilderness to proclaim the nearness of the kingdom of God. Even Jesus was led into the wilderness by the Holy Spirit for forty days where he was tempted by Satan before beginning his ministry. The Apostle Paul spent three years in the wilderness learning from the Holy Spirit. The wilderness most often is characterized as a dry and barren place, a place of physical and spiritual challenge and even death.

Another important aspect of the wilderness is that it is a place that is unable to support abundant life. There is a lack of water, food, and shelter in this environment. There is not sufficient nourishment in the wilderness for life to flourish. God used the wilderness to show man that he is insufficient to provide for himself. Though he may survive, life in the wilderness is harsh and uncomfortable. God contrasts the wilderness with the abundance of his provision. He provided water from the rock, manna from heaven, quail from the wind, and food from ravens and angels to those he led into the wilderness to prove that he is Jehovah Jireh, God our provider. Man left to himself in the wilderness is eventually stripped of the delusions of self-sufficiency and pride and must come to the conclusion that life is sustained by something greater than himself.

WHY THE DISCOURSE ON THE WILDERNESS?

I remind you of the wilderness because that multitude wandering to and fro and kicking up dust is the church. We, that is, you and I and those others called by the name of Christ, have lost our way. The church has become irrelevant in the world. Rather than mirroring the Glory of God, we have become a mirror of the world. We have lost our way, or more precisely, The Way. There are many reasons and events in the course of church history that have allowed or caused the church to stray from the course that Jesus established and become lost. We have followed some of the same paths that the original Chosen followed and have realized the same results. Actually, there are many different wildernesses that make up this barren place. These are the places we will examine as we proceed on this journey. Our Lord has determined that now is the time for the church to shake off the dust, clear its vision, and come out of the wilderness to proclaim his glory.

It is important to grasp the truth of our condition. Unless we realize that we are lost, we will never recognize a need to change direction. This is true of sinners who will never seek a Savior unless they realize they are doomed without him, and it is true of the body unless we realize that we have lost contact with the head. There are definite warning signs that seem to concern us for a time but are then forgotten. This is the dullness that the dust of deception has spread upon us. Though the Bible says that the Lord despises divorce, Christians divorce their spouses as regularly as non-Christians. Church kids are as likely to do drugs and participate in pre-marital sex as are their worldly peers. Sickness and disease are as prevalent in the church as outside it. Our goals and ambitions, material desires and entertainment sources are generally no different than in the secular world. In short, the only real difference in Christians and non-Christians is how they spend the hours of ten to noon on Sunday mornings.

We have escaped into the wilderness within the walls of our buildings. The Lord commanded us to "go into all the world," not to withdraw into the sanctuary consuming programs and seminars that we substitute for real Christian action. The Bible does tell us to study and even to consume the Word, not as a fulfillment of our Christian duty, but to prepare us to go forth to *do* our duty. The criteria for being a "good" Christian today has become church attendance including all the latest seminars and studies. I am reminded of 2 Timothy 3:7, "…ever learning but never able to come to the knowledge of the truth" (KJV).

Though Jesus called us to "be one," Satan has evangelized the church so well that we ignore the obvious division caused by denominationalism. We wander in the wilderness of division, considering those who are of another denomination the enemy. Our real enemy has caused us to divide the kingdom of God into separate kingdoms whose foundations are pride, while he slips through the darkness untouched. While we debate our denominational "revelations," the lost stay lost. The world is confused by the denominational message, and instead of joining the kingdom, they join a side in the debate. God is not the author of confusion. Jesus is not a polygamist; he is not returning for his many brides.

Just as faith without works is dead faith, works without faith are dead. Anyone can do good works. It has been estimated that up to ninety percent of American church donations to foreign missions result in good works but not in bringing the Gospel to the lost. A well-known missionary recently said that before mission money and missionaries came to his country, people went to hell naked and hungry; now they go to hell dressed and well fed. This is an example of the wilderness of dead works. It also includes church buildings that are monuments to architects but obstacles to the lost, towering spires and massive buildings that intimidate rather than invite. Oftentimes millions of dollars are spent on a building that could have been used to reach the lost.

The materialism and greed in our lives and in the message of so many speakers has kept us in the wilderness of stuff as we strive to fulfill the lusts of the flesh in the name of God's abundant life. We sacrifice our children on the altar of greed as we are deceived into believing that more stuff will somehow overcome the lack of parental presence in their lives. We act as if they should somehow be thankful that we have chosen to give them things instead of our time and attention. Our rebellion against the truth of the Word has left us in the wilderness of despair as we find that the rate of divorce, delinquency, and addiction are as high or higher in the church than outside of it. Sadly, we are so comfortable in the wilderness, to consider change stirs rebellion.

What does the church have to offer? Why would anyone be attracted to it? Was the *Wizard of Oz* the truth? Is God the wizard who is just smoke and mirrors to prevent us from finding the god within ourselves? Where is God? Has he lost his power? Is he relevant today? Have the gates of hell prevailed against his church? These questions are as prevalent within the church as outside it. Of course, within they are worded differently and maybe only whispered to our closest friends, but they are still in our minds.

Our Lord, the head of this body, is not pleased by the condition of the church today, but he in his mercy and patience has chosen this time and place to call us out of the wilderness so that we can fulfill the prophetic word of Habakkuk 2:14: "For the earth shall be filled with the knowledge of the glory of the LORD, as the waters cover the sea" (KJV). We are a chosen generation (1 Peter 2:9) called by God to come out and be separate. We are to be aliens and strangers in the earth—in, but not of, the world. We must join that "cloud of witnesses" in Hebrews 12:1 (NIV) so that we can run the race that is set before us.

The wilderness was easy. Finding the way out will

require sacrifice, fasting, perseverance, and prayer, but the reward is great. God has called us to be more than conquerors (Romans 8:37) and over-comers of the world (1 John 4:4). The good news is that each of us is called; the bad news is that many will not listen. The lukewarm Laodicean Church thought they were rich, having need of nothing, but the Lord said they were "wretched, miserable, poor, blind and naked" (Revelation 3:14-17, KJV).

God does not honor the same things we do. Those who hear and hearken to this message will experience the glory of God in their lives; those who don't will be spewed from his mouth. Without doubt, Jesus will have that body of peculiar people—without spot or blemish—who are zealous for good works (Ephesians 5:27; Titus 2:14). Whether you are part of it is your free-will choice.

A Messianic Rabbi I know stated, "The devil has done a remarkable job of evangelizing the church." Satan doesn't rule or lead the church but has little by little introduced deception, pride, greed, and other weapons at his disposal into the body to bring disunity and confusion. In the following sections we will examine some of Satan's tricks so they may be exposed and eradicated. God is bringing the church from the wilderness to glory at this time. How long it takes will depend on how desperate we are to be where he is.

The Wilderness of Tradition

By definition, tradition is the passing down from generation to generation beliefs, behaviors, thoughts, and actions; things are lost and things are added by each generation. Jesus recognized the tendency of man-passed tradition to skew the original intent of God. "You have let go of the commands of God and are holding on to the traditions of men" (Mark 7:8, NIV).

Tradition keeps us separated from each other through denominational pride, racism, style of worship, and even by the clothes we wear. We have rejected the commandment of God to be of "one Lord, one faith, one baptism" (Ephesians 4:5, MKJV), to keep the traditions of men.

Tradition of men has done away with the accountability one brother has for another. Cain asked the question of God, "Am I my brother's keeper?" (Genesis 4:9, NIV). The Word of God emphatically answers this question in the affirmative. Yes. Absolutely yes, we are responsible for one another in the body. Ezekiel brings the message that we are watchmen over one another. He says that if we warn those who do iniquity and they do not repent, they will die, but their blood will be on their own hands. If we see their iniquity and do not warn them, they will die, but their blood will be on our hands (Ezekiel 3:17-21).

"Brethren, if a man be overtaken in a fault, ye which are spiritual, restore such a one in the spirit of meekness..." (Galatians 6:1, KJV). God says to keep an eye on your brothers and sisters, and should they stumble, go to them and lovingly restore them. By doing so we not only save them but save ourselves. Tradition of men says that when our brothers and sisters stumble we should avert our eyes, act as if nothing happened, gossip behind their backs to the whole congregation, and when finally confronted, say we didn't want to hurt their feelings. Matthew 18:15-17 (KJV) gives God's direction for the settlement of disputes within the body.

> Moreover if thy brother shall trespass against thee, go and tell him his fault between thee and him alone: if he shall hear thee, thou hast gained thy brother.

> But if he will not hear thee, then take with thee one or two more, that in the mouth of two or three witnesses every word may be established.

> And if he shall neglect to hear them, tell it unto the church: but if he neglect to hear the church, let him be unto thee as an heathen man and a publican.

If we will not confront our brothers and sisters in the body with all patience and humility, in an effort to restore them, who will? If no one does then we have allowed impurity and ungodliness to take root. "A little yeast works through the whole batch of dough" (Galatians 5:9, NIV).

It is his body; there is no tradition of men that can possibly govern better than the creator. If the body would use the direction of God for mediation of disputes and correction of errant brothers and sisters, the church would began to turn toward the power God intended for it to wield. There would no longer be church splits, and the lost world that watches the behavior of the church would be drawn to the unity.

The devil *has* done a remarkable job of evangelizing the church. When you consider some of the customs in the body today, the evidence is right before you, hidden under tradition. A good example is the tradition of referring to the building in which the church meets as the "*house*" or "*temple*" of God. As this practice has become tradition it has overshadowed the truth that, in fact, it is only a building—no holier or more sacred than any other building. How does this play into the hand of the enemy? First, it gives glory to a building, causing great resources of the church to be expended on its glorious design, construction and upkeep. Second, and more importantly, it gives rise to tradition of keeping this *building* holy rather than the true *temple*, which is the hearts of man. Our children are taught at an early age to behave differently in the *church* building than in other places because it is God's house. They should be respectful here because *this is God's house.*

This behavioral necessity doesn't hold for places like home and school. This gives rise to the false belief that God *sees* your behavior in *his house* but isn't aware elsewhere. From this slick trick of Satan comes the "Sunday only" Christian who gives the lost such a cynical view of Christianity. Our children dress nicely for *church* and *don't run* in *God's house* and think that they have fulfilled their duty to God; then they go out and behave in the same disrespectful manner worldly children do the rest of the week.

As mentioned previously, children who grow up in church are just as likely to be drug users and practice pre-marital sex as their worldly counterparts. No wonder. They are practicing religion the same way their parents do, without regard that it is their body that is the temple of God, not a building

The Pharisees were much like our church today. While they wore the most ornate of robes and praised and prayed long and loud, God proclaimed that their hearts were far from him. Jesus called them "whitewashed tombs," "blind guides," and "sons of hell" (Matthew 23, NIV). We wear our Sunday finest and praise and worship to the latest songs and then go out and live just like everyone else. I wonder what Jesus would call us?

The *real* church is an assembly of true disciples of Jesus Christ who are themselves the temple of the Holy Spirit. The *real* church isn't contained behind the walls of a building but is a light to the world whose good acts bring glory to our Father in heaven (Matthew 5:14, 16). The *real* church behaves the same outside the building as within it—on every day of the week and in all circumstances. Their ethics and practice are the same in business as in their families. They don't cheat on their spouses or their taxes. As a group they are a "city on a hill" whose light draws those lost in darkness. Why? They are aware of their hope of glory—"Christ in you" (Colossians 1:27, KJV)—not in a building.

In the same vein, the tradition of "proper dress" has closed the doors of many local congregations to the poor. Wearing our "Sunday best" clothes goes right along with proper behavior in the "house of the Lord." This tradition of men teaches us to hide who we really are under "proper" clothing. The poor and homeless who may live in the alley behind the church building think they can't attend because they don't have any Sunday clothes. If they do happen to attend, they won't be back because of the looks they get.

My uncle, a Christian man, took my grandmother to a new church she wanted to attend. They went early because my uncle enjoyed attending Sunday school. He participated in the discussion enough that anyone could know he had attended church for a while, but when class was over the teacher came up to him and said, "It's alright that you wore jeans to church today because you didn't know better. Make sure you wear dress pants next time."

Needless to say there won't be a next time at that church for my uncle. Imagine if he had been a lost soul who had finally surrendered to the Holy Spirit's call to attend church. It is unlikely that he would return either. I fear Jesus would speak to us as he spoke in Matthew: "Woe to you, hypocrites! For you are like unto whited sepulchers, which indeed appear beautiful outward, but within are full of dead men's bones, and of all unclean-ness" (23:27, KJV). While speaking of clothing, I remember a young woman who, during marriage counseling, commented that her husband didn't trust her when she left the house. I had to point out that the miniskirt and skin-tight top she had on may have explained his feelings. She let me know with no uncertainty that all her girlfriends at church dressed the same way and that as long as she had a "body like this" she would continue to dress that way. Modesty is not just a church behavior but a Christian lifestyle.

Another tradition from long ago is that the priest, pastor, elder, or whatever the leadership is called in a particular denomination is responsible for all the ministerial duties of the church. He or she is to study the Word, pray for the sick, visit the shut-ins, bring in new members, and be all things to all the members of the local assembly. After the harried minister has done all this, people leave the church complaining they just weren't "getting fed" there anymore. There is nothing in the Word that implies it is leadership that is responsible to perform all these duties. Quite the contrary, the Word tells us that though we are one body, "all members have not the same office" (Romans 12:4, KJV). The next few verses list different ministries in the church that should be performed by those gifted in each particular area.

"Now concerning spiritual gifts, brethren, I would not have you ignorant," Paul begins I Corinthians 12 and then continues to list and discuss the gifts of the Spirit given to each for the "profit of all" (I Corinthians 12:7, KJV). We are all commanded by our Lord to "go into all the world and preach the gospel..." (Mark 16:15, NKJV). We are all told to pray one for another and to confess our sins one to another (James 5:16).

Though the pastor is the shepherd, the whole flock should minister as they are gifted and allow the pastor to lead as he has been called to do. God is no respecter of persons (Acts 10:34). He hears the prayer of all who are righteous (Proverbs 15:29) thus making the prayers of any righteous member in the body effective in reaching God's ear. The church must let the leader lead while each member seeks the Lord for knowledge of his or her ministry gifting and then begins to fulfill his or her calling within the body.

Ministry is a lifelong pursuit. "Let us not be weary in well doing..." (Galatians 6:9, KJV). If we are going to honor our Lord in obedience, Christians must be active in ministry.

The last area of tradition that will be addressed is the method that we expect to change the course of the church. When we seem stuck in a rut or begin to have problems in the body, tradition says it is time for a revival. The truth is that some of that stuff that has died needs to stay dead. We don't need revival. We need reformation. You can't schedule a revival; timing is the work of the Holy Spirit; but you can begin reformation anytime. When the work of reformation is done, revival will probably be waiting right behind it. Reformation means improvement, renovation, reorganization, and rectification. Another synonym is restructuring. We must reexamine the Biblical truths of church organization and purpose and set our hearts on restructuring the church in accordance with the principles of its inception. Examine every office, doctrine, and action to root out man's tradition so that the commandments of God may reign.

Jesus did not establish a church that should die so regularly that it needs two or three revivals a year. The church must be a living organism that thrives on the salvation of the lost and charity to the poor. The walls must be opened so the wind of the Spirit may blow the breath of life across our communities. We have the Gospel, the "good news," the Word of life that the world so desperately needs to hear. The church is called to be that "city on a hill" whose light draws the lost from the darkness. We must be vibrant and alive to seek and save the lost. James said we must be *doers* of the Word.

> But be ye doers of the word, and not hearers only, deceiving your own selves.
>
> For if any be a hearer of the word, and not a doer, he is like unto a man beholding his natural face in a glass:
>
> For he beholdeth himself, and goeth his way, and straightway forgetteth what manner of man he was.
>
> But whoso looketh into the perfect law of liberty, and continueth therein, he being not a forgetful hearer, but a doer of the work, this man shall be blessed in his deed.
>
> James 1:22-25 (KJV)

Reformation creates a body of doers whose lives become ever richer. Remember, faith without works is dead. That is how churches die; they fail to put their faith into action. Throw out tradition and install servant evangelism and watch your church stir from its traditional slumber and come enthusiastically to life—not revived but reborn.

There are many more issues of tradition and ritual imbedded within each denomination. If you will earnestly seek the Spirit of Truth, "He will guide you into all truth" (John 16:13, NIV). He will reveal to you the things of God and the things of tradition. Not all tradition is contrary to the workings of the body, but the enemy of God's church has implanted much that has become tradition, weakened the body, and impaired our vision.

THE WILDERNESS OF SIN

S in, which separates man from God, has crept into the church, and this impurity, like a virus in the physical body, has been systemic in weakening the Body of Christ. In Exodus 16:1 we are told that the nation of Israel was moved into the Wilderness of Sin in response to God's promise that none of that present generation, except Joshua and Caleb, would be allowed in the promised land. There they remained forty years until that whole generation died. The sin that brought the wrath of God on that generation was their failure to recognize God as Almighty God. They doubted God's ability to deliver his promise of victory over the inhabitants of the land he had promised to the descendents of Abraham. There is much sin institutionalized in the church today—pride, greed, inhospitality, and gossip to name a few. The greatest sin is the same as our predecessors—unbelief, fear that God is not able or will choose not to fulfill his promises to us.

This sin goes all the way back to the second commandment, the order not to create graven images or idols to worship. That is exactly what has happened; we have created an image of God that reflects our needs and desires. We would never say that God isn't able, only that he chooses not to keep his promises. We "believe" God has the power to heal but chooses to use doctors instead of healing us directly. This is the creation of an image of God in our likeness. In our headlong rush to attract numbers, we have compromised the holiness of God to make him more palatable to the world. There has been almost a direct inverse relationship between the growth in size and growth in power of the church. We are talking about the spiritual power of the church, not the political power.

2 Thessalonians 2:3 and 1 Timothy 4:1 forewarn that there will be a "falling away" and a "departure from the faith" in the last days.

> For the time will come when men will not put up with sound doctrine. Instead, to suit their own desires, they will gather around them a great number of teachers to say what their itching ears want to hear…They will turn their ears away from the truth and turn aside to myths.
>
> 2 Tim. 4:3, 4 (NIV)

In his messages to the seven churches in Revelation 2 and 3, Jesus warned of infiltration of the churches by heretics and false prophets who taught doctrine contrary to the Word of God. When the church allows heresy to go unchecked and allows doctrine contrary to Scripture to be repeated without correction as an equally acceptable alternative, there can no longer be an expectation of blessing from the Lord. Quite the contrary, he warns that he will remove those churches from his kingdom. The church, as God's army, cannot be tolerant of sin, particularly within the body, and cling to any hope of overcoming the power of the enemy.

The Old Testament is full of stories that show the Lord allowing his chosen to lose battles because there was sin in the camp. God sent his Son to die a horrible death on the cross to redeem us from our slavery to sin. To allow his power to overcome the enemy through those who still live in the sinful nature would make the death and resurrection of Jesus of no effect. Sin and the tolerance of sin in the body separate the church from God and therefore from its source of power. Sin cannot be tolerated but must be exposed, and sinners must be restored in love with all patience and compassion as mentioned earlier. If they fail to repent, they must be treated as "a heathen or a tax-collector" (Matthew 18:17, NKJV).

King David, God's anointed and a man after God's own heart, committed grave sin while ruling Israel. He lusted after another man's wife, seduced her, had her husband killed, and married her (2 Samuel 11). When the prophet Nathan heard of this he went to David and said, "By this deed you have given great occasion to the enemies of the Lord to blaspheme" (2 Samuel 12:14, NKJV). When we who have declared our Christianity continue to act in the sinful nature, we also give the lost room to blaspheme our Lord.

Paul, in Romans 2:24, tells the Jews that because of their sins they have caused the name of God to be blasphemed among the Gentiles. Sadly, the church today has given the enemies of God the same cause to blaspheme the name of Christ because of the sins in the midst of the church. The whole body is held accountable for the actions of its individuals. That is why accountability one to another is crucial in the church. As sin gives reason to blaspheme, so repentance and forgiveness bring out the glory of the church and its head. Jesus warned the churches at Pergamos, Thyatira, Sardis, and Laodicea in Revelation 2 and 3 that he would not tolerate the sin they had allowed in their midst.

The church today must recognize that it is almost inevitable that there will be those in our midst who will use the argument of legalism to justify godlessness and sinful lifestyles. They must be sanctioned with love and patience and taught that salvation is not a license to sin. We must be careful to discern the difference in sinning and living a life of sin. We will all fall in our pursuit of holiness, and God's grace is sufficient to absolve us of our sin, but it does not entitle us to forsake holiness. "If we confess our sins, He is faithful and just to forgive us our sins and to cleanse us from all unrighteousness" (1 John 1:9, NKJV).

There is a balance that differentiates between a repentant believer and one who lives a life of sin without conviction. For example, while on an especially stressful business trip, a husband finds himself tempted by the flirtatious secretary at his client's office. He has been working so hard, and his wife has been so busy with the kids that he enjoys the secretary's overtures. He was only going to have supper with her, but one thing led to another, and he sinned more than he thought he could. The following morning he was dev-astated to even imagine that he could have justified what happened the night before. He bowed right then and begged God to forgive him for the terrible sin he had committed.

Another man, well-respected at his church, often traveled overnight on sales trips. His travels carried him to several familiar locations each year. Each stop had a familiar hotel with familiar women he had come to know through his frequent visits. He often went out with these women and felt that at long as his family didn't know, what harm was there? The second man's conscience had become seared, and he felt no convic-tion. The sin is the same—adultery. The first man, though he must live with his own guilt, is forgiven. The second man is in danger of eternal punishment.

If God is repulsed by sin, surely one who is saved and indwelt by the Holy Spirit will not continue to live a sinful life without a guilty conscience, acting as if Jesus suffered torture and death on the cross so we could continue to sin without consequence. This would be the same as believing that God hates sin until we "repeat this prayer," and then all the things that God hates are now acceptable.

Jesus is coming for his spotless bride, the church, not a sin-stained social gathering.

> Husbands, love your wives, just as Christ also loved
> the church and gave Himself for her, that He might
> sanctify and cleanse her with the washing of water
> by the word, that He might present her to Himself
> a glorious church, not having spot or wrinkle or any

such thing, but that she should be holy and without blemish.

Ephesians 5:25-27 (NKJV)

The church must learn that though we live in the world, we must not be worldly. "Come out from them and be separate, says the Lord. Touch no unclean thing, and I will receive you" (2 Cor. 6:17, NIV) means for us to be in, but not of the world. To restore the sinner in the body of Christ is the responsibility of each person in the church. This must always be done with love, patience, and the right attitude. Using the example above, if either man was found out in his sin, it would be the duty of the church to restore him to both the Lord and his family, if possible. If the family didn't know, it would not be an act of love to reveal the sin to them. The men would both need to affirm their understanding of the sin and to repent of it. If either refused, it would necessitate further action, even expulsion, to preserve the integrity of the church. Even if this occurred, the church should continue to minister truth and love to this individual with the hope of his restoration.

The "Prophets" of the Old Testament were constantly delivering the message of repentance to the House of Israel because they so quickly forgot who their provider was. The modern church, particularly in America, is not unlike the Israelites; we have forgotten our dependence on the Lord and have allowed the world to draw us away from our source. We have not yet molded the golden calf, but we are busily gathering up the gold to smelt. Sin must be called sin and eradicated from the camp. That was the prophet's warning to the children of God then, and he is giving the same warning to his church today. Sin has to be confronted if the church is to come out of the wilderness.

THE WILDERNESS OF INGRATITUDE

Because that, when they knew God, they glorified
Him not as God, neither were thankful; but became
vain in their imaginations, and their foolish hearts
were darkened.

Romans 1:21 (KJV)

As I have studied and listened to my Teacher,
I have come to realize that the foundation of
all sin is ingratitude. Ingratitude is the root of
pride, greed, idolatry, and, eventually, rebellion. We fail
to recognize God as our creator, provider, and sustainer,
so there is no gratitude shown him. Exodus Chapter 32
describes the ingratitude, rebellion, and idolatry of the
Israelites. Though God had delivered them from captivity and slavery in Egypt with mighty signs and wonders, they quickly turned from him and created golden
calves to worship. Luke Chapter 17 relates the event of
the healing from leprosy of ten men, yet only one came
back to thank Jesus for this miracle.

Unfortunately, man is by nature unthankful. We
are born with a selfish nature and must be taught to

share, give, and be thankful. We have to teach our children to share their toys, to say please and thank you. It does not come naturally. When you get irritated by the driver who cut you off in traffic, aren't you really saying that your rights are greater than that person's? Do you fight over the last item on sale? How grateful are we to our employer for hiring us and giving us a paycheck? Doesn't he owe us? How often do we thank God for the air we breathe? It doesn't come easy for us to be thankful and, even if we are, to express our gratitude. Even as Christians we often have conflict within our flesh about charitable giving of our resources, including our time, unless we see the possibility of receiving glory from it. "We work hard for what we have; why should we share it?" This is a common attitude even among Christians. Gratitude proceeds from the recognition that all good things are gifts of God. He formed the earth, its systems, and even formed us in the womb (Isaiah 44:24). He provides the air we breathe and enables our next breath. He is Jehovah-Jireh, our provider, Jehovah-Rophe, our healer, Jehovah-Shalom, our peace, and Jehovah-Rohi, our shepherd. He is the King of kings and Lord of lords, and still we take him for granted.

We begin by thinking we are entitled to God's mercy and grace and from there begin to feel he is obligated to do our will. Each step in this thought process lowers our fear of God and raises our own self-esteem. Pride is planted and begins to flourish. Soon we have accomplished a complete role reversal and begin to act as if God is our servant. We pray for blessings, and when they don't come we blame God. God, however, remains sovereign and continues in his covenant position with man. Though we may have forgotten the "ifs" in this covenant, he certainly hasn't.

Ingratitude angers God. Exodus 32:7-10 (NIV) shows the anger of God toward the Israelites:

> Then the LORD said to Moses, "Go down, because your people, whom you brought up out of Egypt, have become corrupt.
>
> They have been quick to turn away from what I commanded them and have made themselves an idol cast in the shape of a calf. They have bowed down to it and sacrificed to it and have said, 'These are your gods, O Israel, who brought you up out of Egypt.'
>
> "I have seen these people," the LORD said to Moses, "and they are a stiff-necked people. Now leave me alone so that my anger may burn against them and that I may destroy them. Then I will make you into a great nation."

It is only the pleading of Moses that saved them from destruction. Numbers 16:31-33 describes the fierce anger of the Lord toward Korah and his followers because of their ingratitude toward the position God had placed them in.

Psalm 100:4 tells us to "enter His gates with thanksgiving and His courts with praise." "Offer unto God thanksgiving, and pay thou vows unto the most High, and call upon me in the day of trouble: I will deliver thee and thou shalt glorify me" (Psalm 50:14-15, KJV). Our offering of thanksgiving to God along with the keeping of our vows—covenant living, gives us hope of deliverance in our day of trouble. We also find the contrary of this is in Psalm 50:22: "Now consider this you that forget God, lest I tear you in pieces, and there be none to deliver."

How can we imagine that God will honor and bless a people who neither honor nor show gratitude to him? The apostle Paul, in his letter to the church in Rome, addresses the issue of ingratitude and the destruction that follows it.

> Because that, when they knew God, they glorified him not as God, neither were thankful; but became vain in their imaginations, and their foolish heart was darkened. Professing themselves to be wise, they became fools, And changed the glory of the uncorruptible God into an image made like to corruptible man, and to birds, and fourfooted beasts, and creeping things. Wherefore God also gave them up to uncleanness through the lusts of their own hearts, to dishonour their own bodies between themselves: Who changed the truth of God into a lie, and worshipped and served the creature more than the creator, who is blessed for ever. Amen.

> For this cause God gave them up unto vile affections: for even their women did change the natural use into that which is against nature: And likewise also the men, leaving the natural use of the woman, burned in their lust one toward another; men with men working that which is unseemly, and receiving in themselves that recompence of their error which was meet. And even as they did not like to retain

God in their knowledge, God gave them over to a reprobate mind, to do those things which are not convenient; Being filled with all unrighteousness, fornication, wickedness, covetousness, maliciousness; full of envy, murder, debate, deceit, malignity; whisperers, backbiters, haters of God, despiteful, proud, boasters, inventors of evil things, disobedient to parents, without understanding, covenantbreakers, without natural affection, implacable, unmerciful: Who knowing the judgment of God, that they which commit such things are worthy of death, not only do the same, but have pleasure in them that do them.

Romans 1: 21-32 (KJV)

Isaiah 29:13 tells of people who praise God with their lips but whose hearts are far from him. I fear this verse very much describes the praise and worship movement that has become so popular in the church. God desires a purity of worship and praise that goes far beyond entertainment. He desires to be worshipped in spirit and in truth with a pure heart of gratitude for who he is and what he has done. Sometimes there is more glory and honor given the musicians than God. We sing choruses with praise words, but are our hearts truly recognizing the mercy and grace God has extended to us? Is it to worship in spirit and in truth that we sing, or is it just entertainment? God knows our hearts and dwells in the genuine praise of his people but is angered by the hypocrisy of those who sing spiritual words with impure motives.

Ezekiel Chapter 33 speaks of dullness and rebellion

in the people of Israel when God describes the manner in which they hear a prophet of God.

> And they come unto thee as the people cometh, and they sit before thee as my people, and they hear thy words, but they will not do them: for with their mouth they shew much love, but their heart goeth after their covetousness. And, lo, thou art unto them as a very lovely song of one that hath a pleasant voice, and can play well on an instrument: for they hear thy words, but they do them not.
>
> Ezekiel 33:31, 32 (KJV)

The words of God have become entertainment to these stiff-necked people. I would not venture to guess how descriptive this is of our present-day church. How many people leave the church after each service and shake the preacher's hand saying, "That was a good sermon, Pastor." How many of those people are then unable to recall two hours later what the subject of the message was and have no intention whatsoever of changing their lives to correspond with the word of God they have just heard? That is ingratitude, and it is common in the church.

Every one of us has done a favor for someone else who never showed any gratitude. My wife and I recently rescheduled and cut short a much-needed vacation so that I could be present at our facility for a brother who was in desperate need of counseling and restoration. Though we rushed back for him, he never showed up or even called. In ministry we see every day those who take an act of kindness for granted and then turn it into an entitlement, never show gratitude, and then when they are refused for good reason become angry. Is this the way we respond to our heavenly Father who has given us the most precious gift of all? Do we rejoice and thank God in all circumstances for all the good things he has done for us? Can we be as faithful and thankful as Job who in his lowest moment said, "The Lord giveth and the Lord taketh away, blessed be the name of the Lord" (Job 1:21, KJV)?

The path out of the wilderness of ingratitude is really a simple one. "Acknowledge the Lord in all thy ways and he shall direct thy path" (Proverbs 3:6, KJV). Give thanks to the Lord continuously, and praise his loving kindness. Worship him in spirit and in truth and don't let entertainment cloud your praise. "Enter into his gates with thanksgiving, and into his courts with praise. Be thankful to him, and bless his name" (Psalm 100:4, NKJV).

THE WILDERNESS OF PRIDE

It is obvious that every issue that keeps the church in the wilderness is sinful, but some sins need their own discussion. Pride is one of those that deserves its own because of its uncanny ability to deceive. Pride is a slippery sin that manages to fill the vacuum of disobedience by allowing us to act defensively when our sins are exposed. Pride and ego walk hand-in-hand toward destruction. We cannot submit one to another (Ephesians 5:21) or think of others more highly than ourselves (Romans 12:3) if pride reigns in us.

"Only by pride cometh contention" (Proverbs 13:10, KJV). Could this little verse shed great light on the fragmentation of the Body of Christ?

In 1517, Martin Luther posted documents on the door of a Roman Catholic Church and by doing so began the Great Reformation. His documents proclaimed the Gospel—that man is saved by the free gift of grace, through faith, bought by the blood of Jesus at Calvary. Man is saved by grace and not by works, and the act of love on the cross finished the Mosaic covenant and initiated the covenant of grace. "He taketh away the first that He may establish the second" (Hebrews 10:9, KJV).

This knowledge of the Gospel, refuted by the Roman Church to the point of ordering the death of Martin Luther, began the reformation of the church that has made it what we know today. As the ancient Hebrew and Greek scrolls were being translated into modern languages, men became more able to study and seek spiritual guidance to lead the church to be the body that Christ desired. The more revelation knowledge that the Holy Spirit gave to men, the more pride in knowledge divided the Body of Christ. Men like John Calvin, John Smyth, Jonathan Edwards, John Wesley, and others too numerous to mention added their own revelations and methods so the quantity of denominations grew. The invention of the printing press enabled the rapid dispersal of the Bible and books about the Bible into many different hands.

However, even as more men and women than ever were, for the first time, privy to the Word of God, all the Scripture that called for unity—one faith, one body—seemed to fall by the wayside. Denominations began to dwell on the minor differences in doctrine rather than on the great majority of belief they shared, particularly the headship of Christ. The body became fragmented and remains in that state even today. Satan had knowledge of the truth of that proverb, "Only by pride cometh contention" (Proverbs 13:10, KJV). As the Holy Spirit gave revelation upon revelation, pride caused contention between those whose egos were greater than their desire for truth. This is not to accuse any of our predecessors in the faith but to point out that the root cause of today's fragmented church is the sin of pride.

Fragmentation in the body has become so extreme that gifts of the Holy Spirit are labeled demonic even though 1 Corinthians 12-14 plainly explain their origin and purpose. That purpose, by the way, is the edification of the church, not the glorification of an individual. The unpardonable sin, according to Mark 3, is attributing to Satan that which is of the Spirit or, in other words, to blaspheme the Holy Spirit. This practice of declaring any doctrine that differs from our own as demonic has recently spread to the declaration by ignorant and uninformed Christians that the NIV translation of the Bible is the "Devil's Bible," and that the authorized King James translation is the only truly inspired version. Once again, Satan uses ignorance and pride to bring division in the body.

Perhaps the most dangerous form of pride is that which Daniel spoke of in Daniel 5:20: "a mind hardened in pride" (KJV). I will use a true story as an example of this kind of pride. A deacon's wife stood before the body and professed that she had just given her life to the Lord after thirty years of church membership, years as a Sunday school teacher and respected leader of women's ministry, and being recognized by most as a model wife and mother. Her husband had been discussing his lesson based on Galatians 3:24. "Wherefore the Law was our schoolmaster to bring us unto Christ, that we might be justified by faith" (KJV). She heard this Scripture "as if it had been the first time" and realized that she had never recognized that she was a sinner who needed a savior. She had spent thirty years basing her salvation on her own goodness, witnessed by her good works. She confessed that she had felt a tugging in her heart that worried her during altar calls at various times but was too proud to go to the altar. She was worried what everyone would think of her. The tugging had lessened over the past several years, and she gave it little thought. That weekend, however, when she heard her husband speak of salvation by faith, not works, and putting on God's righteousness because ours was like filthy rags, the tugging became unbearable, and she knew she had to repent. For the first time, she realized that her good works would not save her and asked the Lord to be her savior. Thank God for his mercy to this woman.

The dust of dead works clouds our vision. A recent survey showed that, in one major denomination, of 294,000 converts reported in one year, only 14,000 could be found in church a year later. Praise God for the 14,000, but that means 280,000 people are out there somewhere having been told they were "saved" and on their way to heaven. These are the hardest people to bring to the truth of the Gospel because they were told they were already heaven-bound. The only harder group is those of you who have been in church most of your lives but have never sincerely made Jesus your Lord and Savior. You are a good person, do good works, and support the church religiously—like the deacon's wife above, but you have never recognized that you are dead in sin, need the blood atonement of the Savior, and must commit your life to Jesus and be sealed with the Holy Spirit.

How many in every church body are in that condition? How many think they are saved because they repeated a prayer or lifted their hand or filled out a card? How many have never realized that they are sinners bound for hell unless they accept the Lordship of Jesus Christ in their lives? How many don't know that being good, nice, and honest isn't enough to spare their souls? Only God knows the answers to these questions.

Many church leaders believe that thirty percent or more of their congregations are lost and on their way to hell—many because pride has deceived them. Many have hearts hardened by pride, as did the deacon's wife, and no longer hear the call of the Holy Spirit. The Holy Spirit will not force you to be saved; he will only knock. You must open the door of your heart and invite him in. Pride is often the deadbolt that stops God's grace from entering your life.

You probably already know in your spirit that it's you this word is addressing, but pride and fear of exposure keep you from coming forward to confess and repent. You will have to pay the price, but we all are guilty. Our guilt lies before us because we have made God's family so dysfunctional that being honest about our spiritual condition with those in our church may cause us more damage than good. It has been said of Christian soldiers that we are the only army that kills its wounded. Instead we should be so caring of one another that we love and forgive and come to each other's sides in support. The Bible says, "Therefore, confess your sins to one another and pray for one another that you may be healed" (James 5:16, NIV). *Then* the fervent prayers of righteous men avail much.

A body with a large percentage of prideful members who claim to be Christians may have an appearance of Godliness but no real discipleship. Rarely is there a new convert. Rarely are the sick healed, and the gifts of the Spirit for the edification of the body as described in 1 Corinthians 12 are nonexistent.

It is worth repeating that pride keeps us from confessing our sins one to another, a prerequisite for the fervent prayers of righteous men availing much, as we are taught in James 5. Pride stops spouses from agreeing with their adversary and defusing potentially disastrous arguments (Matthew 5:25). Pride causes weak men to lie and lie again rather than accept responsibility and consequences for their actions. Pride causes us to stop fearing God, and the fear of God is the beginning of wisdom.

"God resists the proud, but gives grace to the humble" (1 Peter 5:5, NKJV). Does pride cause resistance from God? Are there long-standing problems in you, your relationships, or your church? The grace of God flows to the humble and stands as a wall of resistance to pride. Humility is the antidote for pride. Submission to others and thinking of others more highly than oneself are scriptural remedies for pride. Humility is not self-degradation but thinking of oneself in a truthful perspective with the overwhelming knowledge that God is the judge and the one who sets the standards. Humility, or humbleness, is the recognition that all you might claim as exaltation is a gift of God. God is our source and our strength and our all in all; there is nothing that we possess that we can claim as our own. His grace toward us is a gift, and we have no place to dwell in pride of his gift. In other words, humbleness and humility come from comparing ourselves to God, not other individuals. Gratitude and humbleness are the only logical reactions to the gift of life we have been given. The Bible says, "Therefore, confess your sins to one another and pray for one another that you may be healed" (James 5:16, NIV). *Then* the fervent prayers of righteous men avail much.

Pride is sin that builds a barrier of deception that will not allow the church to escape from the wilderness. Pride casts the blame anywhere and everywhere so that it will not be confronted. We are fooled into believing that pride is a positive attribute. We even say at times, "All I have left is my pride." Most of the time, if we analyze the situation truthfully, we will find that it is the pride we are holding onto that has cost us everything. For instance, if we are too proud to admit we were wrong, we may lose a friend. If we are too proud to listen to the advice of our financially wise friend, we may lose our wealth. If we are too proud to change our attitude, we may lose our job. If we are too proud to confess our sin, we may spend eternity in hell.

Pride is very deceptive. We can even become proud of how humble we are. If you become upset when someone else receives honor for something you believe you should have been honored for, you have pride in your heart. When the Holy Spirit touches someone in a visible way and you think you should have been touched, you are being prideful. When you expect glory for doing what is right, you are being prideful. Beware of the spirit of pride. Ask God for revelation of pride in your life so that you can bring that part of your soul into submission. Pride can also make you carry burdens that Jesus would carry for you if only you confessed them. "Cast all your anxiety on him because he cares for you" (1 Peter 5:7, NIV).

I was blessed recently to be invited to a large Baptist church one evening to bring several of my students to give testimonies and describe our program. It was an incredible service where one could feel the wind of the Spirit blowing through the sanctuary. As our students testified of God's transforming power in their lives, waves of folks came to the altar in tears for prayer. They would go sit down and another student would testify, and another wave of people would come to the altar. By the time our last student spoke, there was not a dry eye in the place, and a spirit of worship had taken hold. The pastor's wife asked for the microphone and tearfully began to confess to the whole church that on her graduation night she had gone to the beach, drank alcohol for the first time, gotten drunk, and passed out. When she awoke the next morning she realized she had been used sexually but had no remembrance of the event. She then sobbed that she knew God wanted her to confess that night, for someone in the audience, that she had become pregnant from the encounter at the beach and had aborted the baby. Her husband was the only one in the church who had any knowledge of this event. She stood sobbing, asking the church to try to forgive her. I wept as I watched practically every woman in that audience pour to the front and embrace and kiss and kneel with this woman, comforting her as a sister in Christ. Her pride had caused her to carry this burden alone for eighteen years. This church showed the love of Jesus that sets the captive free. Is the love in your church unconditional enough that it is safe to release your pride and confess your sins one to another? If not, is it any surprise that our prayers are not availing much?

Pride ushers in other sins, one of the greatest of which is greed.

The Wilderness of Greed

In the Bible the sin of greed is usually referred to as covetousness. The tenth commandment makes it a law of God that we should not covet that which belongs to another. Covetousness, jealousy, and envy become the sin of greed.

Hebrews 13:5 (KJV) instructs Christians to "be content with such things as you have…" after the warning, "let your conversation be without covetousness." The NIV says, "Keep your lives free from the love of money and be content with what you have."

So how has this sin invaded the church? Through the pride of members, whole bodies become envious of the building that houses the assembly across town and must now waste God's resources to build one of their own that is bigger and more ornate. We don't obey God's direction to bring "all the tithe into the storehouse" (Malachi 3:10, KJV) because we think we have to buy a bigger house, finer clothes, or a new car. My son remarked to me a few years ago that God had performed financial miracles in his life to open the doors for him and his wife to return to college to complete their degrees. I knew they were faithful tithers and reminded them that God made promises to those who tithed. Several months later he called and expressed financial problems. My first question was, "Are you still tithing?" His answer was that they could not afford to since they were in school. They unknowingly had tied God's hands of blessing by their disobedience.

Jesus spoke of the deceitfulness of riches and how they choke out the Word of God. "And that which fell among thorns are they, which, when they have heard, go forth, and are choked with cares and riches and pleasures of this life, and bring no fruit to perfection" (Luke 8:14, KJV). In the church today this has become such a reality. We know of many men and women who early in their ministries had a great love of the Lord and spoke powerful and living messages but have now been so seduced by riches that they have become one-topic speakers. That topic is money, their new god, the thorn that choked out the Word. They still quote Scripture and mention holy terms, but their real message is of riches, usually how we can give them a "seed faith" offering and by doing so become as rich as they are. They spend more time merchandising than preaching the truth of the Word that will set the captive free. There is one well-known TV evangelist that I watched change from a true messenger of the Word to a "huckster" who could use any Scripture as a platform to beg money from his viewers. "Jesus wept." Why? "Because you didn't send me your money." I heard another well-known TV and radio evangelist tell me that the "windows of heaven would be shut to my prayers if I didn't send his ministry a hundred dollars today." I took the chance, didn't send the money, and never recognized any change in God's blessing. They have changed the Word of God into a lie and are exploiting the carnality of the church.

We are forewarned of these in 2 Peter 2:1-3 (KJV). Peter tells us that not only "through covetousness shall they with feigned words make merchandise of you" but that also, because of their pernicious ways, "the way of truth shall be evil spoken of." Peter's prophecy of 2,000 years ago sounds like he had just watched a day of our so-called Christian broadcasting. These evangelists tell their audiences that if they will send their money to specific ministries then God will bless them with wealth. What they call "prosperity ministry" sounds very much like what the Bible calls "covetousness."

Ephesians 5:3(KJV) says, "But fornication, and all uncleanness, or covetousness, let it not be once named among you, as becometh saints." These TV ministries draw money away from the local church and deceive people into believing they are part of this body that is hundreds, if not thousands, of miles away. Members receive no discipleship training, no mentoring, and when trouble arrives they are left alone. One can be sure that the entertaining guy on TV is not going to come visit you in the hospital or grieve with your loss. That entertaining guy only wants your money and uses the name of God to get it. But we can't place all the blame on others; we are the ones who send our money hoping to receive riches. We must ask, is there Scripture that says God won't heal unless you send someone a "seed faith" offering? No, there isn't.

James Chapter 5 gives warning to those who have laid up treasures in the last days, who live in luxury and have withheld wages to the harvesters. God has blessed no one with wealth for his own profit but that he may bless others. Do you realize that there are many people who might not be able to go to some foreign land as missionaries but would gladly work full-time in domestic missions if only their basic expenses were covered? These are the harvesters, along with the thousands of men and women who work tirelessly in the kingdom of God in pastoral positions at poverty levels because of the greed of "Christians." There are many churchgoers who maintain two houses so they won't be inconvenienced by the weather, while homeless families huddle under bridges to survive. Christians buy top-of-the-line automobiles for every driver in the family and drive by other Christians who struggle to buy shoes.

Feeling a little angry at these words? My guess is it isn't the Holy Spirit in you that is riled up. If Jesus were here now, I wonder if he would have a private luxury jet and travel with bodyguards the way some of our TV evangelists do. I wonder if he would live in the finest houses in the finest neighborhoods. If he saw one of the "least of these," I wonder if he would turn his head or throw some loose change at him.

Do you realize that Jesus should be here? He should be seen daily in the lives of his body doing the things that he did. Remember the WWJD movement? What a powerful thought and message that was brought forth in the book *In His Steps*. What became of it? It became a merchandising and fashion movement instead of a move of the Spirit. Instead of contemplating the actions of Jesus, we let the world know we were Christians by wearing bracelets and other ornaments tagged with the WWJD logo. Unfortunately, what the world saw was more hypocrisy than ever before. But some people made a lot of money exploiting the thought. This also reminds us of the prophecy in 2 Peter 2.

Greed isn't just about material things; it also involves our time. When was the last time you truly ministered to anyone? Have you been too busy or greedy with your own interests to consider anyone else? Jesus made this issue a litmus test for Christians. "Verily I say unto you, inasmuch as you did it not unto the least of these, you did it not to me. And these shall go away into everlasting punishment...." (Matthew 25:45-46, KJV). Do you see that Satan has deceived the church into believing that charity is an option? Greed is deadly in the individual and in the body.

There are massive, ornate church buildings in this country a stones throw from impoverished neighborhoods. I once sat in a battered storefront sanctuary from the rain and cold with about thirty homeless folks whose lives had been ravished by poverty, drug addiction, and mental illness as we watched a well-known preacher on TV tell us that if we would only send $50 he and his prayer warriors would pray over our letters. The anger, dejection, and depression that engulfed the room showed how little understanding this religious greed had of the plight of men. The fact that this plea for money came from a beautiful cathedral with a golden candelabra and the richest of furnishings made matters worse. Matthew 5:45 tells us that God makes the sun rise on the good and the evil and sends rain to both the just and unjust. Don't mistake the fruit of your labor for a blessing from God. In other words, your prosperity doesn't mean God is pleased with your greed.

The verses in Matthew 25 encourage us to feed the hungry, give drink to the thirsty, clothe those who are naked, and take in the stranger. They also instruct us to visit the sick and go to the prisons. Though money is an important issue in some of these situations, the real issue is love and humility. "Do not think of yourself more highly than you ought" (Romans 12:3, NIV). To do this and to love our neighbor as we love ourselves (Luke 10:27) are two admonitions that Christians must embrace to have a charitable heart. By participating in the ministry to the poor, hungry, homeless, naked, sick, and imprisoned, we are more able to humbly praise God for his blessing and to recognize his grace directed toward us. More importantly, we obey his command to love our neighbors as ourselves.

Charity is the antidote for greed, and humility is the antidote for pride. We are an affluent people, and it is easy for us to write a check to absolve ourselves of any responsibility to get involved. But if you really want to receive a heart-changing blessing from God, give him your time. Go visit one who is elderly, take a poor child shopping, volunteer at an AIDS hospice or a drug rehabilitation center, or join in a prison ministry. Your heart will swell with the presence of God, and you will find that, though you were a blessing, it was you who felt truly blessed.

When we give of ourselves to the service of the

Lord, we begin to love one another as he loves us. We grow in maturity as doers of the Word and become closer to the Lord. We become content with what we have, and this is a godly state. "But godliness with contentment is great gain, for we brought nothing into this world and it is certain we can carry nothing out. And having food and raiment let us be therewith content" (1 Timothy 6:6-8, KJV). This changes us, our families, our friends, and, above all, our church. As our church changes by the service ministries of the body, our community changes because now the light is reaching the darkness. Forget storing up and begin giving out, and see the glory of the Lord in your life.

There was church in North Carolina that began meeting at the local YMCA. Over time their building fund swelled so that they were in a position to begin building a building. Instead the pastor spoke to the board along the lines of WWJD, and the church decided to use their building money to fund low-income housing in their community. The community saw Jesus in that decision, and the church grew until it could no longer fit in the YMCA and had to build its own building. There are many lessons to be learned from this course of action.

God honors those who honor him. He blesses those who bless the lost sheep. He will always out-give the greatest giver. He blesses the selfless and resists the selfish. The lost are drawn to Christ's love as seen in putting the welfare of others above our own selfish interests.

The Wilderness of Deception

The Apostle Paul admonished Timothy in his second letter:

> Preach the Word; be prepared in season and out of season; correct, rebuke and encourage— with great patience and careful instruction. For the time will come when men will not put up with sound doctrine. Instead, to suit their own desires, they will gather around them a great number of teachers to say what their itching ears want to hear. They will turn their ears away from the truth and turn aside to myths.
>
> 2 Timothy 4:2-4

In other words, there will be a time when men will welcome the deception of the world to justify trying to serve both God and materialism. They will follow supposed "men of God" who teach that grace is license to do as we please with no consequences. These lukewarm

Christians will be comfortable hearing about the love of Jesus but will close their ears to teaching about the blood of Jesus. They will ignore the significance of the blood as the love in action. They will accept Jesus as their Savior but will reject him as Lord of their lives. That we were bought with so great a price might make us feel obligated, so we choose to shy away from those kinds of sermons. Deception soothes our conviction so that we can be "lukewarm" and believe that God owes us blessing because we are not cold. After all, at least we come to church on Sunday.

Jesus said, "I wish you were either cold or hot, but because you are lukewarm, I am about to spit you out of my mouth. You think you are wealthy and don't need a thing. But you do not realize that you are wretched, pitiful, poor, blind and naked" (Revelation 3:15-17, NIV). My, my, how different is the mind of God from the mind of man. It is God's desire that we see through the eyes of truth, yet we continue to walk happily in the blindness of the world's deception.

> Do not be deceived: God cannot be mocked. A man reaps what he sows. The one who sows to please his sinful nature, from that nature will reap his destruction; the one who sows to please the Spirit, from the Spirit will reap eternal life.
>
> Galatians 6:7

Deception is one of the enemy's greatest weapons. He used it against Adam and Eve in the Garden of Eden, against Jesus in the wilderness, and is still using it against the church today. Jesus warned of this deception in Matthew 24:24 (KJV): "For there shall arise false

Christs, and false prophets, and shall show great signs and wonders; insomuch that, if it were possible, they shall deceive the very elect." Their doctrines will sound Biblical, their appearance will be without reproach, and they will be embraced by the leadership of many churches, but you will have a knot of doubt arise within your spirit—probably something you can't put your finger on or even express, just a subtle something that bothers your spirit. That something is the Holy Spirit guarding the elect. The Holy Spirit is the only one that can keep the elect through this age. If you choose to ignore these warnings that the Holy Spirit places within you, you may well be deceived. If your spirit is troubled, leave. God will not cause you to miss a blessing he has for you because you used wisdom and fled from confusion. Your spiritual well-being is far more important than the message of any man or manifestation of whatever spirit.

There is a growing movement, even among mainline denominations, to accept a worldview that Christianity isn't the only way to salvation—that all people of faith have a right to expect eternal life with God. (We are tempted to add, "Whoever he, she, or it may be.") After all, Christianity claims to be the *only* way, and this is a very intolerant view. What right do we have, or so the argument goes, to claim that our way is not only the right way but the exclusive way? We are told, "If we are going to exist in peace on this earth with our neighbors who hold different faiths than us, we need to compromise and realize their faith is as real to them as ours is to us."

This seemingly innocent dribble covers a cruel

reality that unfortunately is true. We don't know what Christianity or being a Christian means. This ignorance makes the truth a lie and deception appear inviting. This is the falsehood Jesus spoke of when he said, "Many false prophets will appear and deceive many people" (Matthew 24:11, NIV). To compromise and embrace a worldview that on the surface seems to promote peace and unity brings to mind that proverb, "There is a way which seemeth right unto a man, but the end thereof are the ways of death" (Proverbs 14:12, KJV). To lose sight of the fact that Jesus said, *"I am the way, the truth and the life. No one comes to the Father except through me"* (John 14:6, NIV), is to reject the whole plan of salvation that Jesus died on the cross to fulfill.

If you are a Christian, you must reject any other method of eternal life with God except the one proclaimed in the Bible by Jesus Christ. That does not make us intolerant. Everyone else can still believe whatever they wish. Recognize that the goal of the world is to coerce Christians not just to be tolerant of their beliefs but to grant them equal validity to those we hold sacred. By doing so, we would make of no effect the whole cornerstone of our faith, that Jesus is the Son of God and our only hope of salvation and eternal life through the atonement of his shed blood. To die for the Gospel is far better than to live in peace on earth by the denial and compromise of its precepts.

"Blessed are you when people insult you, persecute you and say all kinds of evil against you because of me. Rejoice and be glad, because great is your reward in heaven" (Matthew 5:11, 12, NIV). These are the prophetic words of Jesus at the Sermon on the Mount. Be prepared to face persecution and suffering. As our Lord suffered, so shall we. We may find it is easier to die for Jesus than to live for him in the days to come. God's people have always been persecuted because we are strangers in a strange land. We are God's people and, in fact, his children. "I will be a Father to you, and you will be my sons and daughters, says the Lord Almighty" (2 Corinthians 6:18, NIV). We are as much the enemy of the world's kingdom as our firstborn brother, Jesus, was. He showed us, by example, that though we may be insulted, suffer, and even be put to death; we will triumph in the end. Death has no hold on God's children. By the resurrecting power of God, we will join our Father in heaven for eternity. "O death, where is thy sting? O grave, where is thy victory?" (1 Corinthians 15:55, KJV).

False doctrine is almost always built on Scripture by deception of interpretation or dwelling on one Scripture and excluding the balancing word. Those skilled in deception can quote Scripture that appeals to our lusts and ignore Scripture that calls us to repentance. For example, there are those who for personal reasons claim the sin of Sodom was "inhospitality" rather than "immorality," though Jude 7 makes us quite aware that sexual sin was the real cause of that city's destruction. Those who preach the "prosperity" doctrine seem to be quite unaware that in all his mention of money or wealth, Jesus never spoke of either as worthy objects of desire. To the contrary, he taught that it was easier for a camel to pass through the eye of a needle than for a rich man to enter the kingdom of God. There is doctrine that appeals to those who believe nothing is free, even salvation.

"If you don't have to earn it, it isn't worth having," they say. They are the ones who proclaim certain types of food or dress or days of the week are more esteemed than others. These often include those who promote racial hatred in the name of God and Christianity. Others, out of fear of confronting sin in their own lives or the lives of their leadership or big financial supporters, use the Gospel of grace as a license for immorality. Many of these have "a form of godliness but deny the power thereof, from such turn away" (2 Timothy 3:5, KJV).

Beware of those who speak love and tolerance. "There is a way which seemeth right unto man, but the end thereof are the ways of death!" (Proverbs 14:12, KJV). Long suffering, patience, and love are all fruits of the Spirit, but tolerance leads to death. It is the counterfeit of grace. The doctrine of tolerance is itself immoral because it is a deception. Tolerance is based on the notion that there is no absolute truth or morality— there can be no right or wrong, good or bad, or judgment and correction. Everything is based on individual opinion that has no meaning past the next individual opinion. The only absolute in the whole tolerance message is that tolerance should be applied to everyone except Christians.

Our truth is based on grace. We recognize that we all deserve judgment but because of the grace of God are justified. The place for tolerance in the church is to recognize that, right or wrong, those who are outside of the church have a right to serve their master, whoever he, she, or it may be. Within the church we are unified by the grace of God and not by the deception of tolerance. Every wall and division of race, gender, nationality, and circumstance was removed at the cross, that one place where every Christian's path came together. We are not united by tolerance but by the grace of God through the blood of Jesus.

It is God's will "that we should no longer be children, tossed to and fro and carried about with every wind of doctrine, by the trickery of men, in the cunning craftiness of deceitful plotting" (Ephesians 4:14, NKJV), yet we fail to study God's word to be filled with truth. We become gullible to the deception of false teachers and prophets because we are ignorant of the truth in God's Word, trusting everyone except the Holy Spirit to give us truth and wisdom. A recent survey showed that only 5% of professing Christians have read the whole Bible. If you don't know what God says, how can you be sure that the latest "Christian" book isn't just a slick trick of the enemy to deceive you? I can guarantee you that I have read books touted as Christian that actually qualify for the "Pits of Hell Award." The Apostle Paul warns us about these authors. "Such men are false apostles, deceitful workmen, masquerading as apostles of Christ. And no wonder, for Satan himself masquerades as an angel of light. It is not surprising, then, if his servants masquerade as servants of righteousness" (2 Corinthians 11:13-15, NIV). How do you know if you are being fed truth or deception if you don't have the truth of God's Word in your heart where the Holy Spirit can bring it to your remembrance?

The kingdom of God does not conform to the traditions and institutions of man. If you don't make the effort to have knowledge of God's kingdom in which you dwell, you are open to deception. The Word of God, the Bible, is the only place we have to gain the knowledge of the truth. I would not trust my eternal condition to the words of any preacher unless I checked his message against the Truth in God's Word. Be like the Bereans who were "of more noble character than the Thessalonians, for they received the message with great eagerness and examined the Scriptures every day to see if what Paul said was true" (Acts 17:11, NIV). This failure to seek knowledge of the truth has allowed deception to compromise the power of the church and keep it wandering in the wilderness.

The critical thought is that we are not of the world. We are called to be separate, different. We are called to be light, not just another religious group that fills the world with more rules and regulations. The church Jesus established was commissioned to go into the world and bring the good news of freedom through salvation. "It was for freedom that Christ has set us free" (Galatians 5:1, NIV). Do not be entangled by religious rhetoric that tries to combine Christianity with the ways of the world or religious fervor. We are called to be different, in but not of the world.

> You adulterous people, don't you know that friendship with the world is hatred toward God? Anyone who chooses to become a friend of the world becomes an enemy of God.
>
> James 4:4 (NIV)

Therefore come out from them and be separate,

says the Lord. Touch no unclean thing, and I will receive you.

> 2 Corinthians 6:17 (NIV)

Do not conform any longer to the pattern of this world, but be transformed by the renewing of your mind.

> Romans 12:2 (NIV)

We all have the choice to make: kingdom of God or kingdom of the world? "Choose you this day whom you will serve...but as for me and my house we will serve the Lord" (Joshua 24:15, KJV). It is a choice that must be made. Grace is not a license to sin. Paul clearly states:

> Do not be yoked together with unbelievers. For what do righteousness and wickedness have in common? Or what fellowship can light have with darkness?.... What does a believer have in common with an unbeliever? What agreement is there between the temple of God and idols?
>
> 2 Corinthians 6:14-16 (NIV)

Have you made a choice? Do you feel like an alien in this world? Do you yearn to go home to be with your Father? Does the ungodliness all around you vex your spirit as Lot's was vexed in Sodom and Gomorrah?

THE WILDERNESS OF
WORLDLINESS

Worldliness is a catch-all word for pursuit of and devotion to the things of the world rather than heavenly affairs. Another word that describes this state is carnality, which speaks of a pleasing of the flesh rather than the spirit. Both of these words can be used to describe the church in the wilderness. The kingdom of heaven is contrary to worldly attitudes. As a matter of fact, the two are almost diametrically opposed. For example, the worldview of success is power, prestige, and wealth, while the kingdom view is humility and service. The first worldview respects the accumulation of material possessions, while the kingdom view respects the accumulation of souls.

Worldliness and Godliness cannot exist together.

Ye adulterers and adulteresses, do you not know that friendship with the world is enmity with God?

> Whosever therefore will be a friend of the world is
> an enemy of God.
>
> James 4:4 (KJV)

The holiness of God is so offended by the sinfulness of the world that the two cannot be in the same room together, certainly not in the same body. The Holy Spirit that abides in the heart of a Christian is grieved when that Christian desires things of the world. That's when our consciences begin to try to get our attention to direct us in another direction. If we don't heed this prick by our conscience and continue in worldliness, our conscience can become seared, and we may no longer recognize the call to repentance. So many of the body have ignored the voice of the Spirit and become seared in their consciences that we hear, "It's only a movie, only a song, only entertainment. It's just a date. It's not like I'm going to marry him/her. Who's going to know? Everybody does it. Just once isn't going to matter. Well, I'm not as bad as so-and-so." All these excuses are straight from the pit but have become a part of our communications because our seared consciences no longer protect us from evil.

A deacon of a church recently told me, "God wants us to be rich, and then the unsaved will be drawn to us. Who wants to join a bunch of poor people?"

We have traded the good news of salvation for the supposed good news of prosperity. The attitude seems to be that if we can be more like the world then the world will like us more. Does this attitude make us a city on a hill or a light to the world? Or does it make us just like the world? We forget that the Holy Spirit calls sinners to repentance, and it is unlikely he will call many to a place that is so worldly even demons are comfortable there. The church was established to bring the light of the Gospel into the darkness of the world. This light will make the world want to hide because of the holiness that is its source.

1 Corinthians 3:3 (NKJV) gives a test for carnality in the body. "For you are still carnal. For where there is strife, envy and division among you, are you not carnal and behaving like mere men?"

Does your church have strife, envy, and division? If it does, you are attending a carnal church. What can you do? Be a peacemaker and be blessed (Matthew 5:9). Forgiveness, peace, love, faith, and holiness are the elements of Christianity that overcome the strife and division in carnal man. If these elements are not manifest in your life and your church, you have a carnal nature and do not know the fruit of the Spirit (Galatians 5:22, 23).

As the world has criticized the church, the church has given in to the world. We have already spoken of the false image of God we have created to please ourselves and the world. The church has become tolerant of sin to please the world and has thus become irrelevant as a beacon of hope. The world didn't like the truth of the Gospel, the shedding of the Savior's blood to resurrect us from our state of death in sin, so we toned it down to make them happy, and still they taunted us. No good god would send someone to hell, so we either did away with hell or changed the nature of God to appease the complainers. They were happy with a god that was kind and good and helped their finances and marriages, so that is what the church gave them. Everyone likes to be entertained, so the church found new ways to entertain, and the numbers grew. New seminars and programs developed to occupy and entertain, and the numbers grew again. Some of the programs actually did good things outside of the walls of the church building. But the Gospel didn't go out with the programs; we didn't want to "push" our belief on anyone else. The truth is we can't share the good news that is not in our hearts.

One quick example, a church begins to collect and give out food to the poor and hungry. This is obviously a good thing to do, but the bottom line is the poor remain poor, and the hungry have their hunger quenched for a day or two. If this cycle continues until those needy people die, they may go to hell a little fatter than they would have before they were given food. We must take to heart our obligation to preach the Gospel. If we confront these people in a loving way when they pick up food, pray with them, and tell them the truth of the Gospel, then those needy people will have the opportunity to experience the loving concern of a Christian that may change their eternal destiny. Our first responsibility is to preach the Gospel. It is great to do good things, but it is Godly to spread the Gospel.

The world is searching for something different, and we are giving them more of the same. The Gospel is radical teaching, and the church should reflect this radical message. Man has searched for eternal life throughout recorded history, and we have the key to the quest. Carnal man rejoices in life and fears death. To the Christian life is nice but "death is gain" (Philippians 1:21, NIV). Mortal death gives way to eternal life.

But when this corruptible shall put on incorruption, and when this mortal shall put on immortality, then will take place the word that is written, "Death is swallowed up in victory. O death, where is thy sting? O grave, where is thy victory?"

1 Corinthians 15:54-55 (MKJV)

We are commanded to "come out from among them, and be ye separate" (2 Corinthians 6:17, KJV) so the world can see the difference in us. Our difference is to bring glory to the Father and to attract the lost to the light of Jesus in us. When the church becomes too much like the world, the differences blur and we lose our attraction. Somehow the enemy has convinced us to believe the lie that worldliness will attract the world. The world has placed its big cozy arm around us and is slowly squeezing the life out of the church, and we feel comfortable. A church without Gospel conviction but with fun programs may indeed generate big numbers. Unfortunately, these numbers reflect moths drawn to the delight of the light, only to die in its brilliance.

We must come out of the wilderness of worldliness by putting on the cloak of his holiness so that the world may see the true glory of the Giver of Life. Then the lost will be drawn to the brilliance that never dims and the light that leads to eternal life.

The Wilderness of Apathy

Apathy means we just don't care, are unconcerned, and are indifferent. Another description would be that we just don't really think it is our business or responsibility. How many people gave their lives to the Lord at your church last year? I was at a church a couple of years ago that was being honored as the church with the highest per capita rate of baptisms for the year. This was a 500 member church that had baptized five people. We are surrounded by the lost and dying that have never made Jesus their savior. Does anyone care? Many of you have family members you know would go to hell if they died today. Do you care? Crack houses are operating next door. Do you care? Nursing homes are overfull with no one visiting to spread some cheer and help break the loneliness. Do you care? Children are being abused. Do you care? We live in a very sick and sinful world. Do you care? Jesus does. That is why he died such a horrendous death on the cross, because he cared.

Can we really believe we are following our Lord, Jesus Christ, and refuse to notice what is happening around us?

The contrast between the chaos of the world and peace of true Christianity is so great today that our opportunity to make a difference by *doing* the right things is better than it has ever been. People are anxious, stressed, and fearful about world events. Crime and violence cause us all to be careful and even cold. We are warned that "Because of the increase of wickedness, the love of most will grow cold" (Matthew 24:12, NIV), so we should not be surprised by apathy. Wickedness around us does not justify the church to withdraw within the walls and ignore the plight of the lost and needy. Eleven of the twelve disciples died tortuous deaths because they recognized that we are at war against the forces of evil in the world. Ephesians 6 tells us that we must put on the full armor of God to combat the enemy. Our heritage has many songs that remind us of the battle, though they are seldom sung anymore. The "Battle Hymn of the Republic" and "Onward Christian Soldiers" are two that readily come to mind.

The church was apathetic in the 1940s toward the onslaught of Adolph Hitler in Europe, particularly toward the Jews. Where were the Christians? In my generation, we watched millions of men, women, and children being slaughtered in Rwanda. Where were the Christians? The AIDS epidemic swept America. Where were the Christians? Each of these battles was ignored by the apathetic church.

I volunteered for hospice training at the height of the AIDS epidemic and expected Christians to be well represented in the class of ten or so. I was the only one. Several Christian friends told me it was a homosexual issue. No, my blind brothers and sisters, it was a lost and dying issue. It was an opportunity for the church to shine a light into darkness from which we excused ourselves because it affected *them* not us. It was a time that our apathy caused us to miss a great opportunity to witness the love of Jesus to the homosexual community.

Unless we take the Gospel into the highways and byways, the lost will stay lost. Apathy isn't an option for Christians. We are commanded to preach the Gospel and to spread the light—all of us. Whether we pray and intercede, speak and interpret tongues, prophesy, teach Sunday school, or whatever other task we may do, we are not excused from preaching the Gospel and spreading his light. You can pray until the cows come home, but unless someone speaks the Gospel people will not be saved. If every Christian brought only one person a year to the knowledge of the saving grace of Jesus, there would be millions saved each year besides those who hear evangelists. There are exponentially more Christians than there are evangelists, though we should all be ministers of God's grace. Your church would double in number each year if only each one reached one. The devil has worked hard at convincing us not to care, to let it be someone else's problem, and to be so concerned with our own lives that we really don't notice anyone else's. Next time you are in a public place like the grocery store or sports stadium, stop and consider for a moment how many people around you probably do not know Jesus. If you really want to stop being apathetic, ask God to burden your heart for the lost. Eternity is forever. Care where your family and friends are going to spend it.

Apathy is killing the church. Our gifts and talents are useless and wasted unless we care enough to use them. Our hearts become harder and harder as we ignore the suffering around us. What did Jesus do? Wasn't he moved by love and compassion to minister to the sick and oppressed? Didn't he go to the outcast and set them free? Why don't we? Do we really not care? If we do care, let's go out and try to bring them in, in the name of Jesus.

MYSTERIES

There are two mysteries mentioned in the Bible referring to the church that we must understand to advance the kingdom as we are required to do. The first is found in Colossians 1:27 (KJV): "To whom God would make known what is the riches of the glory of this mystery among the Gentiles, which is Christ in you, the hope of glory."

We are born of flesh, and those who accept Jesus as their savior are *born again* of the Spirit (John 3:3-7). The Spirit of Christ moves into the empty place in our hearts and makes that his residence. He is our only hope of glory. Our own righteousness is as filthy rags to the Holy One.

The second mystery is found in Ephesians 1:9-10, 22-23 (NKJV).

He made known to us the mystery of His will...to bring all things in heaven and on earth together under one head, even in Christ...And God placed all things under his feet and appointed him to be head over everything for the church, which is his body, the fullness of him who fills all in all.

This is the church, the gathering of all those who are called to a oneness in the body of Christ. Though the body is comprised of individuals, it is called to function as a single unit. "That all of them may be one, Father, just as you are in me and I am in you. May they also be in us so that the world may believe that you have sent me" (John 17:21, NIV). This is the prayer of Jesus for his disciples and for those who would believe in him through their message. In other words, though we may be saved individually, we are saved into the body of Christ. There is no salvation outside that body.

From this point in his ministry, the message of Jesus was to his body. Understanding the oneness of the body with the head, Jesus Christ, draws us into the knowledge of the unity with Jesus and one another that he expects from his church.

It is within this oneness that we must learn to glorify God—as a body, not as individuals. It is the body that is the bride. We must learn to love one another because that is how the lost will know we are his disciples.

In order for us to be the "glory of the Lord that covers the earth as the water covers the sea" (Habakkuk 2:14, MKJV), we must recognize that the body of Christ must be molded together based on Holy Spirit revealed truth and not fragmented by all the various devices of the enemy. God has given us space and time to repent, and now is the time to move forward out of the wilderness in which the church has wandered and become that glorified bride that Christ can reclaim as his own. This process will include the great "falling away" (2 Thessalonians 2:3, MKJV) that the church is already experiencing, a coming together of all the remnants, and a church marching together dressed in the full armor of Christ shining his glorious light throughout the world.

The church is living in some of the hardest times since it was established. In many parts of the world Christians are being put in prison, their land is being confiscated, children are being torn from their parents, beatings and torture are common, and even to be murdered for professing the name of Jesus is not uncommon. Recently in Australia, while we watched the international news of the region, we saw the heads of Christians stuck on the ends of poles, paraded through the streets, in countries north of us. We know that in China many are beaten and imprisoned for his name's sake. In Chad and Sudan, Christian girls and women are forced to become sex slaves to their captors. These are just a few of the more heinous examples of the price that professing Jesus Christ costs our brothers and sisters in other parts of the world. For the most part we just suffer being called hypocrites, "hate mongers," intolerant, and bigots. Studies say that there have been more Christian martyrs in this century than in all the previous history of the world combined. This is assault from the world, certainly not an unexpected event.

"And you will be hated by all nations because of me" (Matthew 24:9, NIV). The attack from the inside, from those we thought were brothers and sisters, is the hardest for us to take. But this, too, is taking place, just as Scripture tells us it will. "At that time many will turn away from the faith and will betray and hate each other...Because of the increase of wickedness, the love of most will grow cold" (Matthew 24:10, 12, NIV).

The Apostle Paul continued Christ's message that the body is a corporate entity. There is no provision made in the Bible for Lone Ranger Christians. Most of the Apostle Paul's message was to the church. The general theme was how the individual was to conduct his life to conform to the Body of Christ. The purpose is so the kingdom of God may be advanced in one mind and one accord. There has to be conformity to one doctrine of faith to avoid the fragmentation that characterizes the church today. We are not supporting the idea of the oneness of "people of faith" but are speaking of the concept of one God, one Jesus Christ, one faith. We have to embrace within the body the new command of Jesus that we love one another.

In order for the church to show the world that we are in fact the Body of Christ, we must surrender our pride to the Holy Spirit and let him work that miracle of unity in the body. Each individual Christian must make a conscious decision to let the Holy Spirit guide him or her into unity one with another in Christ. There is tradition in each of us that needs to be examined in the light of Holy Spirit revealed Scripture. Has doctrine based on tradition or denomination built a wall between parts of the body? Has pride turned this wall from paper to concrete? Will we surrender our will and pride to God's will and righteousness, or will we be left behind as the church is unified and beautified? Maybe we should consider adding a new sign to our church sign that says, "The Body of Christ meeting at (whatever church)" so at least unbelievers would consider the unity of the body.

It is important to recognize that the corporate church is made up of individuals. The whole can only function to the extent that its parts are committed. For example, in most local churches there are a few who are submitted, surrendered seekers of the Lord's will for their lives. These bring in their tithes, give of their time, and seem to be the ones that the whole burden of the function of the church falls upon. Charles Spurgeon, a great and well known man of God in the mid to late 1800s, was very influential in church building during his lifetime. He was a prolific writer and published over 700 sermons. He recognized a problem that is as common in the body today as it was in his day.

"The Church of God will always have ill times so long as a few people are left to do what should be done by all the redeemed" (C.H. Spurgeon, *Sermons on Revival*).

We are familiar with a 500-plus member church. Approximately 250 to 300 will attend church on Sunday morning. This number falls to eighty on Sunday night and forty to fifty on Wednesday night. A once-a-month prayer service will be attended by six to fifteen. What we have here is a very small group of people carrying the weight of the majority. We have a church that struggles financially, families that struggle spiritually, and a pastor and staff that are so busy putting out flash fires they have little time to spend in the presence of God. Then the members selfishly complain that they are not getting fed. They don't pray earnestly, don't read, much less study, the Word of God, don't tithe, don't visit the sick, don't set an example for their children or peers. They don't consider those in the church that do all these things without a word of criticism or a moment's complaint. This is not an unusual church but a church that is considered active and alive. Only God can know for sure the condition of a man's heart, but Jesus says, "Every branch in me that beareth not fruit, he (my Father, the husbandman) taketh away" (John 15:2, KJV).

Let's stop for a moment and consider another point of view. What do we look like to the unbeliever, to the un-churched, to the lost we are supposed to be seeking? We are reminded of Paul's words to the Jews who were supposed to be the examples of God's chosen in that age: "For the name of God is blasphemed among the Gentiles through you" (Romans 2:24, KJV).

The question must be brought up, are we bringing glory or blasphemy to the name of the Lord? Paul brought this accusation against a corporate body, but it had earlier been brought against an individual who had a very visible position in God's kingdom. Nathan said to King David, after revealing his sin against God with Bathsheba, "By this deed you have given great occasion to the enemies of the Lord to blaspheme" (2 Samuel 12:14, MKJV).

I bring up these two Scriptures to remind us that the snake is always watching us, both corporately and individually, for evidence to thwart our mission to his lair. We are always accused, as Jesus was, by our own profession of beliefs so that we may be branded hypocrites. This is so those who are aware of our failure may be deceived into believing that we are no different from them, and they can be honest about it. We must be aware that as church members and professing Christians, we are always being watched and judged. We are witnesses whether we choose to be or not. How we respond to this knowledge will determine whether we glorify or blaspheme the church and ultimately the name of God to those around us. Remember, *we* are the church!

As we consider this question of our appearance to those to whom we are commissioned to bring the Gospel, perhaps we should consider the negative question. How does the church blaspheme God? What are our attitudes and behaviors that give cause to those we seek to be indifferent to our plea? Maybe another question will produce some new thought. Do we look like Jesus? If we are his disciples, we should walk as he walked. Jesus told us how those we come in contact with would know that we are his disciples "that we love one another" (John 13:35, NIV). Love enables us to forgive, understand, be patient, and be united. It creates in us humility, submission, unselfishness, peace, and joy. These are the attributes that attract the lost to our Gospel. It's not because our building is new or because we have a good choir or the best softball team. It's because they see in us the hope of peace, joy, and unity that man desires in his soul. Division shatters this hope, causes confusion, and makes our claims of the Gospel appear to be a lie. The only division that God ordains is our division from the world. We must embrace the mystery of Christ in us so that we may function as Jesus intended as one body with Christ as our head.

The Way Out

Then I saw a column moving toward me, five or six people wide, stretching back to the throng. The music becomes louder, more triumphant. I was taken back to the original viewpoint, but higher. Now I can see the path all the way into the wilderness and back to the throng. The front of the column has come around the mountain in the background and is coming straight up the path between the other two mountains.

It is easy to sit back and criticize, to see only the negative and ignore the positive aspects. But because God's people are called to a higher standard (1 Peter 1:16, KJV), we have to be concerned about the negative. As Jesus addressed the seven churches of Asia in Revelation 2 and 3, he acknowledged their positive traits but still warned of their judgment because of the negative. God does not balance good and evil and reward us by preponderance of evidence. He calls us to be holy, without blemish or wrinkle. As is often said about sin in Scripture, "A little yeast works through the whole batch of dough" (Galatians 5:9, NIV). The Body of Christ must strive for perfection through the power of the Holy Spirit who is sent to mold us into the likeness of Jesus. God has sent his grace to enable us to overcome. Grace has been misunderstood and misused as a cover for sin, but grace is truly a gift to help us overcome not cover up.

Earlier I told you of a vision of a crystal spire that was filthy and how a snow-white cloud covered the spire. When the cloud had moved from the spire it was spotless, shining and sparkling in the sun. Then a voice came from the cloud and said, "I will clean my church."

This vision shows the unilateral action of the head to cleanse his body. This is the action of 2 Thessalonians 2:3(KJV): "for that day will not come except there come a falling away first." This represents the apostate in the body that Jesus will allow to fall away. They will be caught up in their own deception that exchanges the truth for a lie.

In this time, the church, in its quest to be appealing to the world, has so lost touch with its roots that it has become that entity spoken of in 2 Timothy 3:5 that has a "form of godliness but denies the power thereof" (KJV). It has failed to obey the directive of 2 Corinthians 6:17 to come out from among the worldly and be separate. Therefore Jesus has allowed the cleansing through apostasy to begin. This is the great falling away of 2 Thessalonians. The world will see a separation between the true bride and the counterfeit. Unfortunately, many so-called Christians will embrace the counterfeit because its worldliness will feel more familiar to them. There will also be a renewed call to holiness in the church that remains so that the light of God will shine throughout the earth. This is the glory that will cover the earth as the water covers the sea. This will be the bride, radiant and glorified, awaiting her soon-coming Bridegroom.

We see mainline churches that have embraced homosexuality as an acceptable alternative lifestyle. Some have declared that Jesus isn't the only path to heaven. The cry for tolerance resounds from the top officials in some denominations. At least one denomination has a high-level office whose main function is to proclaim the "Christian" pro-abortion platform. There must be a separation of the true church from this apostate counterfeit. Jesus has declared his intention to do just that—to cleanse his church.

Leviticus 15:31 is an insight or precursor to God's intent for his people. "You must keep the Israelites separate from things that make them unclean, so they will not die in their uncleanness for defiling my dwelling place, which is among them" (NIV). We know that since and because of the cross, the dwelling place is no longer *among* us, but *in* us. This is why we are called to come out and be separate and touch no unclean thing, so that we might have life and not die in our sin. There must be a separation from worldliness. The church that has embraced the "unclean thing" must repent or fall away; there is no in between.

To embrace the unclean thing means to embrace

worldliness. In its headlong rush to be accepted by the world, the church has compromised holiness. We have tolerated sin in the body so long that it has become institutionalized. Our hearts and consciences have been seared to accept means that are ungodly to reach ends that are worldly. Big numbers, big revenues, big programs, and big buildings are the criteria used to judge the effectiveness of the church rather than the commitment to holiness. Bigness does not impress an awesome God. Broken and contrite hearts do.

Let me interject at this time that the "holiness" that is called for in this work is not the legalism that caused the word to have a bad name. There was and is much in the "Holiness Movement" that is far from holy. With a blind eye to loving kindness, long suffering, and patience, the participants in the holiness movement placed legalistic rules including dress codes, use of makeup, forceful spousal submission, and other outward regulations to rule and control their constituents. The fruits of the Spirit were forgotten and replaced with harsh judgment. Being overly judgmental and unloving in applying rules is not holy. Holiness herein means to be Christ-like and display the fruits of the Spirit (Galatians 5:22, 23). I once had the opportunity to take a young couple to visit their critically-ill newborn in a children's intensive care hospital. Though they were part of a local church, no one from their church had offered to take them on this sixty-mile trip. On the way to the hospital, the young man asked if he could listen to his pastor's tape from Sunday morning. This tape was so full of legalism and judgment that it wounded my soul. I asked the couple if this pastor had ever been over to visit or pray for their baby and they said no. On the way home, after praying diligently for this poor child, the father asked if I thought it was okay to drink wine. When I carefully explained the difference in a glass of wine with dinner opposed to drinking to get drunk and explained about not doing anything that could cause your brother to stumble, he blew up in anger and accused me of not being a Christian. I just dropped the issue and continued driving. The next day, Sunday, his wife called quite upset and asked if my grandmother and I could come over right away. When we arrived, she met us at the door with a black eye and bruises all over and told us that her husband had beat her up because she came out dressed in a very modest pant suit for church. He didn't think women should wear pants to church. An elder from his church arrived shortly and agreed with the husband. They described themselves as holy. I believe the Lord would consider them far from it.

There is also another group who are hanging by a thread, those who are lukewarm and like vomit in the mouth of God. It is only his patience that gives time for repentance before you are spewed from his presence. Your time is short; your judgment is to be swallowed up in the wilderness by the chasm of apostasy unless repentance comes quickly.

Finally, there is the church that has lost its way and has wandered in the wilderness so long that the dust of deception has blinded it to its plight. It has been oppressed by legalism, fooled by doctrines of cheap grace, and deceived by false teachers and prophets. As the dust covers their eyes, so it dulls their faith and destroys their hope.

There is nothing in the world that is not a part of the struggle between good and evil. Nothing else really matters. God would have us be ever-mindful of the ongoing conflict, and the snake does everything in his power to conceal any conflict at all. He would much prefer us to be absorbed in entertainment, material things, time schedules, illness, debt, and any other diversion that would keep us occupied in things of the flesh rather than the things of God. When our time on earth is over, whether through death or the ending of this age, nothing will be of any consequence except our spiritual response to the battle of flesh versus Spirit. All things—money, fame, and success—will suddenly be of no concern. Our whole life will be weighed by one question: did we accept Jesus as our Lord? The answer will determine eternal life or eternal death. And just as the snake attempts to conceal conflict, he will do anything to influence the church to be deceived, to be caught up in politics, social issues, programs, seminars, fundraising, building programs, and every other good-sounding diversion, to deter it from its real calling of spreading the Gospel.

We are in a spiritual war. As the secular world is at war against terrorism, so are we in a war against evil. There are some similarities between the two. Neither has a well-defined enemy; they don't wear specific uniforms. They both operate covertly. They seem to know where the cracks in security are; they know our weaknesses. They both use our freedom and liberty to advance their causes.

The enemy can use without conscience any method to attain its goal, while we are constrained by moral decency to shun becoming evil. The enemy does things that are too horrible and ugly for us to imagine until they happen. There is a reason for these similarities. The evil side of both wars is under the command of the snake. He has heightened his spiritual conflict with the church, God's kingdom, and he has begun a secular war against the nation that most represents Christianity—the United States. As we have said, we are at war. We know that we are already the victors; Jesus won that victory over 2,000 years ago. But we must be careful not to become casualties of the final mop-up battles. In the secular world there will always be wars and rumors of wars until the Lord ends this age. In the spiritual world the war began in the Garden of Eden, has continued nonstop ever since and will not end until the King of Kings reigns over the earth.

We are warned in Revelation 12:12 that the devil has come down to earth with great wrath because he knows that his time is short. His time is very short, therefore the battle of this age is very intense. But never forget, we are the winners! God, who declared that the gates of hell would not prevail against his church, has sent messengers into the wilderness to open the eyes of his people and lead them to victory! He has sent a plan with these spokesmen that will signal the victory of the body, the glory of the Lord, and the final destruction of the world's kingdom.

As the Lord begins to cleanse and purify his church, we should consider our role in the process. We should start with a new commitment to commitment, surrender to submission, and recognize our inability to do neither without the power of the Holy Spirit. His plan begins by urging those who will hear to listen to the voice of the prophet Jeremiah and call on the Lord. He has promised to answer us and tell us great and mighty things that we don't know (Jeremiah 33:3). After we have obeyed and called on him, we are directed by Jeremiah to "Stand at the crossroads and look; ask for the ancient paths, ask where the good way is, and walk in it, and you will find rest for your souls" (6:16, NIV). The crossroads is where the lost church is standing. We ask you, Lord, where is the ancient path?

God showed me that we, his people, have arrived once again at the historic crossroads that go back into the history of his people for centuries and generations. Adam and Eve stood at this place, Moses stood here, Joshua was here, Daniel was here, and David was here. Peter was here, and so was Martin Luther. We could go on and on. This is the test of free will. We as individuals and as a people called by his name must choose the path we will travel. If our choice is the Lord Almighty, he has already given us the way to him.

In 2 Chronicles 7, as Solomon dedicated the temple to the Lord, the Lord made a covenant with his people. He made this covenant with them at a time in history when he was reasonably pleased with them. But God reminded them that, though they may fall out of his graces as they had done many times before, there was a way to return. This is the promise of 2 Chronicles 7:14 (NIV):

If my people, which are called by my name, will

humble themselves and pray and seek my face and turn from their wicked ways; then will I hear from heaven and will forgive their sins and will heal their land.

This is a covenant promise of God to his people. Is the remedy that simple? Jesus said that his yoke is easy and his burden light (Matthew 11:30). It is simply spoken and pretty simply understood, but there must be a problem because we are where we are. The answer is in the directive from Jeremiah to take the ancient path to find rest for our souls (Jeremiah 6:16). The key word is path. A path is something to be followed. It is also a place. We must stay on the path now to see where the path takes us. Let's see if we can follow the ancient path of this covenant of God and get to his glory.

We must recognize that this is a conditional covenant ("*If* my people..."). A conditional covenant means there is a condition that must be fulfilled before the promise takes effect. It is a conditional covenant between two parties, God and his people, more specifically those of his people who are called by his name. For the church—those who are called by his name—this is a promise to restore the body to the glory that was intended from its inception. There is a healing or restoration awaiting us *if* we will fulfill our part of the covenant.

Our part is to humble ourselves and begin to pray and seek his face and to turn from our wicked ways. Let's break that down and see what it means. The best definition of *humble* used in this context is to submit. To submit to the lordship of God, to place God above everything else in our lives including family, careers, hopes, dreams, and self. We must recognize the awesomeness and sovereignty of an Almighty God. If we can begin to recognize and fear his true awesomeness, humbleness becomes relatively easy. Humbleness is the cure for pride. We have already shown how destructive pride is in the church and in individuals. Pride comes first and then the fall. James says in the fourth chapter of his book that if we will humble ourselves before the Lord, he will lift us up (verse 10). As pride is the first step before the fall, humbleness is the first step before we are lifted up.

How do we humble ourselves? We begin by renewing our mind to things of the Spirit rather than the old habits of materialism and worldliness. We learn to think of others more highly than ourselves (Romans 12:2-3). We learn to be submissive (Ephesians 5:21, NIV). Be like Jesus; take on the position of a servant. Remember, the King of kings and Lord of lords, the darling of heaven, the Son of God, the Messiah, lowered himself to our level and then bowed down and washed the feet of his disciples. How can we not humble ourselves before so great an example? I will give you one more Scripture without comment other than to let the Spirit of Truth speak to your submitted heart.

> If I then, your Lord and Master, have washed your feet; ye also ought to wash one another's feet. For I have given you an example, that you should do as I have done to you. Verily, verily I say unto you, the servant is not greater than his lord; neither is he

that is sent greater than he that sent him. If ye know these things, happy are ye if ye do them.

John 13:14-17(KJV)

Both pride and humility are incredibly powerful weapons; the weapon you choose will determine which side you support.

If we humble ourselves and begin to pray, we will start to turn things around. The word for that process is repentance. This is not prayer to bring our needs and desires before the throne but prayer to seek his face—prayer to find out his plan and will for our lives and for the church corporate. "To seek his face" means to get in step with God, to let his concerns become our concerns, to find out what he is doing and join him there. In this light, those things about us that are contrary to the holiness of God will be exposed so we will be made aware of what parts of our lives need repentance. That is why this order is important. We must humble ourselves, pray, and draw near to God so that his light may illuminate the darkness in us. When we see ourselves in his holiness then our spiritual healing begins (Hebrews 10:10, 14). This is our part of this covenant between God and his people.

So what prevents us from walking daily in this covenant? We will not humble ourselves to anyone or anything we don't fear. We have created a god in our own image that may be worthy of respect in our eyes, but we don't fear him, because we are *his* creator. We have filled him with love, goodness, and mercy but no holiness or judgment. He is sort of a senile, old lovable guy whom we can pray to and thank for the stuff that we know we have really provided by our own efforts. He is like the mascot of our social religious club, a good example to tell our children stories about. He has a special power to guide and direct doctors but no independent power to heal. In other words, we have created a safe god—one we can control.

Jesus asked in Luke 18 if he would find faith on earth when he returns (verse 8). The sad answer is not enough. We seldom have faith in that which we do not fear. We believe that Jesus recognized that as time progressed and man became more blessed by God, man would cease to fear him. The more God blessed the Jews, the more likely they were to become prideful in their blessings. The less needy they became, the more likely they were to turn to created gods. The more prideful they became, the more their fear of God diminished. Are we that prideful? Have we lost the fear of the Lord?

The answer is yes, but God has not lost his power or position. He still rules with power and might. We have been deceived and have created our own golden calves, but God calls us, even now, to break down the false gods we have created and return to the ancient way. He reminds us that he is the high and Holy God that lives in a high and holy place and, through the blood of Jesus, in broken and contrite hearts.

Fear him and humble yourselves before him. Let the Holy Spirit lead you to repentance so he will forgive your sins and heal your land. Our all-powerful, all-knowing, ever-present God has promised to us, his people, that if we will obey him, he will surely forgive our sins and heal our land. When he forgives our sins we are made perfect, holy, and righteous in his eyes. Everything past is forgotten, and we are in perfect harmony with the God of the universe. When he heals our land he heals our marriages, families, relationships, bodies, finances, and churches. If the Body of Christ begins to follow the path directed by the Lord, and all his covenant promises of forgiveness, healing, financial security, and family unity started to be manifest in our lives, I believe the world would be drawn to us.

This covenant is perpetuated in those who are called by the name of Jesus, since we are now the temple of God. If we become humble, pray, seek his face, and repent, the wandering will cease. Find out what the church is supposed to do and begin to do it. This will prepare us to begin the trek out of the wilderness. It's just that simple. Jesus has already done the work; all we have to do is walk in the way he showed us. This way will lead us along our life journey to our destination in eternal communion with our creator. Remember, coming out of the wilderness is only the beginning of the journey.

Winning the War

The front of the column has come around the moun-
tain in the background and is coming straight up
the path between the other two mountains. I can
see the individuals in the column. They look as if
they have been through a mighty conflict—clothes
in rags, blood stains on their bodies. I am drawn to
their faces; there was no conflict there. These were
the faces of over-comers—strong, courageous, beam-
ing with hope. The music became louder and more
victorious.

Put on the whole armor of God, that you may be
able to stand against the wiles of the devil. For we
wrestle not against flesh and blood, but against prin-
cipalities, against powers, against the rulers of the
darkness of this world, against spiritual wickedness
in high places. Wherefore take unto you the whole

armor of God, that you may be able to withstand in
the evil day, and having done all, to stand.

Ephesians 6:11-13 (KJV)

It is a war, and our enemy has no integrity. He will
use everything in his power to defeat the church
of Jesus Christ. We are God's army and must be
properly trained and equipped for the battle. This is
the purpose of the body, many parts making up one
unbeatable force.

There are some called to relay the Word of our commander, some to lay out the plan, some to recruit new
soldiers, some to watch over the lives of the troops, and
some to teach warfare tactics. All these work together
for the equipping and encouragement of the army of
God's kingdom (Ephesians 4:11-12). Unlike most warfare we are not only guaranteed victory but victory
without a single casualty, if we obey our commander.
Our Lord has dominion and authority over the leader
of the opposition. The Lord says we are *more than conquerors through him* (Romans 8:37) and that *all things
work together for good to them that love him* (Romans
8:28). Our victory is assured because the God in us is
greater than the enemy in the world (1 John 4:4).

Even though we know that in the end we will be
victorious and overcome the powers of the world, we
must still stand as resistance. Our quest is to obey the
order of our commander-in-chief to go into all the
world and preach the Gospel and make disciples of all
nations. Our enemy will try to distract us from our goal
using every weapon in his arsenal: selfishness, greed,
tradition, pride, lust, fear, doubt, and all sorts of sin. His

greatest weapon, death, has already been neutralized by
Jesus through the Resurrection, but the devil still tries
to use the fear of death to resist us. We are an army that
has at its disposal every necessity for victory. Our Lord
has given us salvation to overcome the fear of death,
truth and righteousness to protect us from deception,
faith to shield us from every attack, and his Word as
our weapon to counterattack (Ephesians 6:11-17).

However, it is an all-volunteer army given free-will
to disobey and compromise with the enemy. We have
been infiltrated with propagandists from the enemy
who have lessened our resolve and even persuaded some
of us that the war has ended. We have been offered rich
rewards to lay down our weapons and compromise our
goals. We have been convinced that the wilderness is
the promised land and have grown comfortable in the
dust.

As in the past, God has preserved a remnant who
have not lost their first love and whose zeal remains.
They have or will hear the messengers who are calling them out of the wilderness. As they begin to follow the ancient path out of dry, barren places, others
will come to their senses (Luke 15:17) and return to the
truth. This will arouse the enemy to step up his warfare,
but those awakened will destroy him with the power of
the Word. This will be an army of over-comers unlike
any known in all history. They will move into the world
and conquer it in the name of their God. Nothing will
be impossible to these who have stood the test and recognized their position. They are the Chosen, a Royal
Priesthood, Sons of the Most High God and his dwelling. Signs and wonders will follow them, and the Glory

of the Lord will shine upon them. The sick will be healed, the lame will walk, the blind will see, and even greater things than these will they do. It is this church that will become the bride of the Lamb and will *fill the earth with the knowledge of the Glory of the Lord, as the waters cover the sea* (Habakkuk 2:14).

The Details

On the slopes of the mountains I saw small bushes
and trees, barely large enough to provide shade. All
over the slopes, hidden under these plants, were people. I wondered why I hadn't seen them before. They
were covered by ragged tents and blankets, and I
could see that most of them were wounded, crippled,
and nearly dead. Then I saw some of those in the
column begin to move into the scrub, to direct those
who could walk and to carry those who couldn't, out
to join the march. The column never slowed but continued to move forward. I was drawn to one older
man who used a homemade crutch as he tried to get
down the slope. Soon two from the column came
and placed this man's arms on their shoulders and
helped him to the ranks. It seemed significant that
his crutch fell to the ground as the two supported
him. When they reached the column the two contin-

*ued to support this man. I watched as his face began
to glow and take on that same look of victory and
hope of those around him. He grew stronger with
each step and was soon marching on his own.*

After the church becomes humble, begins to pray, and seeks the face of the Lord, repenting of its sins, the first love of the body will begin to manifest, and zeal to serve will soon follow. Those in the body who have not chosen to be a part of the repentance process will arise and try to suppress and discourage change. If the leadership recognizes the true church, they will support the change while counseling and teaching the others. The end result will be a church within the church or an exodus by those who were not prepared to serve the Lord. Remember the parable of the tares in Matthew 13:24-30. The tares were allowed to remain in the field.

As long as these members do not cause strife, there is always the possibility that they will repent and join the army. If there is conflict within the body, it must be met with openness and truth. We can no longer allow the Body of Christ to be blasphemed for the uncorrected behavior of unrepentant members. Correction and restoration must always be carried out with patience, longsuffering, and compassion but must be carried out nonetheless to preserve the holiness of the body.

The church that emerges from the wilderness will be united by placing the things of God above the desires of men. That important question, "What did Jesus do?" serves as a guide to direct our paths. The admonishment to "pray without ceasing" (1 Thessalonians 5:17, KJV) will keep the church in tune with the Holy Spirit so that he may lead it. This church will be a self-sacrificing body that expends its energy and finances outside the building by reaching out to the hungry, helpless, homeless, abused, and lost souls in the community around them. Ministry will replace entertainment as the fulfillment in our lives. It will be a group that, like Jesus, judges the inward and not the outward appearance of man.

There will be a hunger to know and draw nearer to our Lord, to truly be his servant. We will begin to have a relationship and communion with Jesus and be in unity with one another. There will be a coming together of like-minded believers like never before when we come to the full understanding of the oneness of the Body of Christ. Ministry will flourish, causing the light of the church to reflect our Father's glory and so draw men to him. We will then go out into all the world, starting with our families, friends, and neighbors, and spread the Gospel, our message of hope, to the hopeless around us.

Most importantly, we will continue the war, clothed in the full armor of God, for the souls of men. The enemy will be set on his heel by this fresh and vibrant force and will attack with everything at his disposal. Because this will be a new army he isn't prepared for—humble servants of the Lord, full of love and compassion, doing what Jesus did. In fact, this army will be doing *even greater things* in the name of our Lord. This is the church that Jesus established and proclaimed that the gates of hell would not prevail against. This is the church that the enemy has always feared would arise because he is powerless against it.

This is the church that will hear the trumpet blow, calling it to meet our Lord in the clouds. "Now is the time," says the Lord of Hosts. "There will be no other."

Arise, shine, for your light has come, and the glory of the Lord rises upon you. See, darkness covers the earth and thick darkness is over the peoples, but the Lord rises upon you and His glory appears over you. Nations will come to your light, and kings to brightness of your dawn.

Isaiah 60:1-3 (NIV)

Epilogue

Let us love one another. The victorious church will be seen as a body that leaves the safety of the inside of the building and goes into the surrounding community to show God's love, mercy, and grace to those who need it. Some will make the effort to find the lost sheep that have been hurt and have left the assembly. Compassion will flow from the fountain that has for too long poured out judgment and unforgiveness. Pride will be replaced with humility, and we will begin to think of others more highly than ourselves.

We will be seen going into the scary places, by the power of our God, to rescue the lost and dying. Our brothers and sisters will be able to trust that if they are wounded we will surround them with our presence and our prayers. We will learn to be slow to anger and quick to forgive. We will worship in "spirit and in truth." No longer will we be tossed by the winds of doctrine but will be anchored by our knowledge of God's Word.

Come out! Come out of the wilderness. Come out of materialism. Come out of arrogance and pride. Come out of the building. Come out of your comfort zone. Come out into the Glory of God and be led by his Spirit. Come out from among them and be a separate people.

Let us be those who spread the knowledge of the Glory of God so that it covers the earth as the waters cover the sea!